MW01046350

Hiking

Oregon's

Three Sisters
Country

by
Bruce Grubbs

FALCON®

HELENA, MONTANA

A FALCON GUIDE

Falcon® Publishing is continually expanding its list of recreational guidebooks. All books include detailed descriptions, accurate maps, and all the information necessary for enjoyable trips. You can order extra copies of this book and get information and prices for other Falcon® guidebooks by writing Falcon,® P.O. Box 1718, Helena, MT 59624 or calling toll-free 1-800-582-2665. Also, please ask for a free copy of our current catalog.
Visit our web site at http:\\www.falconguide.com

©1997 by Falcon® Publishing, Inc.
Helena, Montana.

All rights reserved, including the right to reproduce this book or parts thereof in any form, except for inclusion of brief quotations in a review.

Printed in the United States of America.

All black-and-white photos by the author.
Cover photo by Jon Gnass

Library of Congress Cataloging-in-Publication Data

Grubbs, Bruce (Bruce O.)
    Hiking Oregon's Three Sisters country / by Bruce Grubbs.
        p.   cm.
    Includes bibliographical references (p.   ).
        ISBN 1-56044-567-X
        1. Hiking—Oregon—Three Sisters—Guidebooks.   2. Three Sisters
    (Or.)—Guidebooks.   I. Title.
    GV199.42.072T574   1997
    796.51'09785'8—dc21   97-9745
                                                                 CIP

CAUTION

Outdoor recreational activities are by their very nature potentially hazardous. All participants in such activities must assume the responsibility for their own actions and safety. The information contained in this guidebook cannot replace sound judgment and good decision–making skills, which help reduce risk exposure, nor does the scope of this book allow for disclosure of all the potential hazards and risks involved in such activities.

Learn as much as possible about the outdoor recreational activities in which you participate, prepare for the unexpected, and be cautious. The reward will be a safer and more enjoyable experience.

 Text pages printed on recycled paper.

CONTENTS

CONTENTS

The Hikes

CONTENTS

CONTENTS

ACKNOWLEDGMENTS

I wish to thank all the people and organizations who have made this book possible. I especially want to thank Stewart Aitchison for getting me into the writing business and providing valuable advice along the way; Duart Martin for hiking with me, putting up with my photography, and doing invaluable proofreading; and Rob Martin for sharing a fine backpack trip in the Oregon Cascades. Thanks also to my longtime hiking companion, Doug Rickard, for reviewing the hike descriptions. I wish to thank Steve Soreth of the Willamette National Forest for reviewing the section "Making it a Safe Trip" and coordinating the review of hikes among the ranger districts.

I'd also like to express my appreciation to the personnel of the Oakridge, Sweet Home, Blue River, McKenzie, and Detroit ranger districts who reviewed hikes in their districts. Their comments helped ensure the accuracy of the book. Finally, I wish to thank Randall Green, my editor, and the rest of the folks at Falcon who worked with me and made this book happen.

OVERVIEW MAP

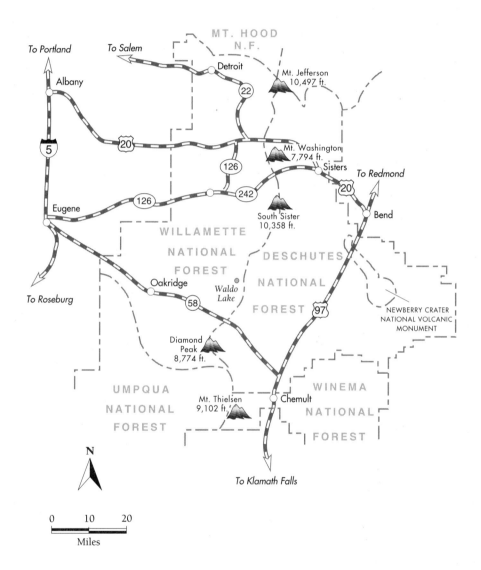

To Portland

To Salem

MT. HOOD N.F.

Detroit

Mt. Jefferson
10,497 ft.

Albany

22

5

20

Mt. Washington
7,794 ft.

126

Sisters

To Redmond

20

126

242

Bend

Eugene

South Sister
10,358 ft.

WILLAMETTE

NATIONAL

FOREST

DESCHUTES

NATIONAL

Oakridge

Waldo
Lake

To Roseburg

58

FOREST

97

NEWBERRY CRATER
NATIONAL VOLCANIC
MONUMENT

Diamond
Peak
8,774 ft.

UMPQUA

NATIONAL

FOREST

Mt. Thielsen
9,102 ft.

Chemult

WINEMA

NATIONAL

FOREST

N

To Klamath Falls

0   10   20

Miles

LEGEND

Interstate	15		Forest/Wilderness Boundary	— — — — — — — ..
U.S. Highway	66 134		Campground	▲
State or County Road	47 190		Bridge	⏝
Forest Road	4165		Ranger Station	🚩
Interstate Highway	⇒		Cabins/Buildings	■
Paved Road	⇒		Peak/Elevation	9,782 ft.
Gravel Road	⇒		Falls	—⫽—
Unimproved Road	======⇒		Pass/Saddle	)(
Trailhead	○		Gate	•—•
Main Trail			Map Orientation	N ↑
Secondary Trail			Scale	0 0.5 1 Miles
Cross Country Trails			Overlook/Point of Interest	▫
River/Creek			Sand Dunes	
Lake				
Ditch				
Spring	⟋			

USGS TOPOGRAPHIC MAPS

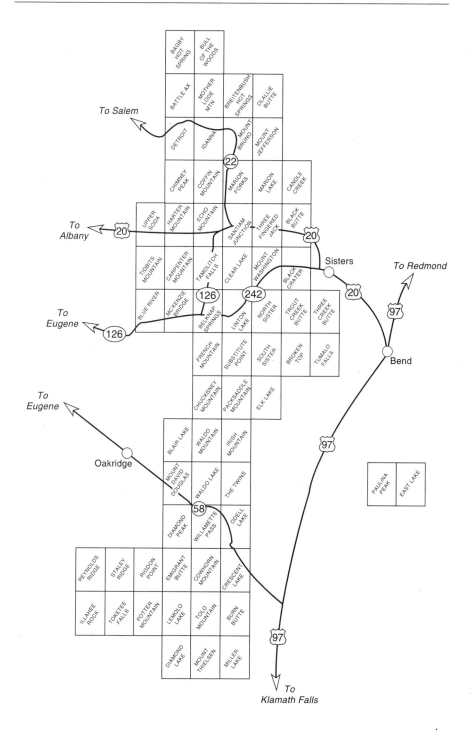

Olallie Butte reflected in Monon Lake.

INTRODUCTION

Oregon's Three Sisters country is an excellent area for hiking and backpacking, as generations of Oregonians and visitors already know. For those who are new to the area, or want some new ideas, this book covers the central Oregon Cascade Mountains from the Olallie Lake Scenic Area and Mount Jefferson Wilderness in the north to the Mount Thielsen Wilderness in the south. This is a highly accessible backcountry region. Nearly all trailheads can be reached in a couple of hours from cities in the Willamette Valley and central Oregon.

One of my primary purposes in writing this book is to introduce people, especially non-hikers, to this exceptional country. Accordingly, I emphasize shorter and easier hikes, with easily reached trailheads. The rating system for the hikes is also slanted toward beginners. Many of the hikes described here can be enjoyed by people who don't think of themselves as hikers. Avid hikers with small children may find the easier hikes more appropriate for a family outing. Of course, there are also challenging day hikes and backpack trips in this book.

I have hiked all of the featured hikes in this book and have made every effort to ensure the accuracy of this information. Be aware, however, that trails and roads sometimes are rebuilt, damaged by storms, or closed; that trailheads sometimes are relocated; and other changes may occur in the wilderness. Before leaving for your proposed hike, check with the ranger station listed with each hike for the latest road and trail information.

WHY HIKE?

I have enjoyed backcountry walking and hiking ever since I can remember. Though I also ski, mountain bike, climb, and kayak, I return to hiking again and again. I find that walking allows more opportunities to look around and really see the country I'm traveling through. I also find the individual and leisurely speed of hiking and backpacking is a great complement to the faster pace of modern civilization. I almost always emerge from a hiking trip refreshed and ready for new challenges in the manmade world. Hiking also provides a great opportunity to indulge other interests, such as geology, birding, fishing, or photography.

Walking in the wilderness is not just a matter of "picking 'em up and putting 'em down!" Most novice hikers try to go too fast, then find themselves out of breath and stopping frequently. The group should move at a speed that allows easy (not breathless!) conversation among all members. Long hikes, especially uphill sections, should be paced so that rest breaks are needed only about once an hour. That's not to say that you shouldn't stop at scenic viewpoints or when you find something else that is interesting. But if you find yourself taking a great many breaks, you're probably going too fast. Keep rest stops short so that you don't become chilled. It's harder to get going after a long break.

As you walk, always pay attention to the stretch of ground immediately in front of you. Hazards such as spiny plants, overhanging sharp branches, and sunbathing rattlesnakes are easy to miss if you only have eyes for the scenery on the horizon. On the other hand, daydreaming is an important part of hiking. There are always sections of trail that aren't that interesting. Experienced hikers can let their minds wander far away but still pay attention to the trail underfoot and the route ahead. Or they can focus on aspects of the environment, such as bird song or identifying trees from a distance by their general shape. Both techniques let the miles pass almost unnoticed.

Hikes taken with young children should have extremely modest goals. A day hike of a few hundred yards may be far enough. Children find all sorts of interesting things in a small area that their parents would never notice.

THE OREGON CASCADES

GEOGRAPHY

The Cascade Range starts in northern California and extends north across central Oregon into Washington and Canada. It is the highest range in Oregon, reaching 11,235 feet at Mount Hood. The Cascades intercept much of the moisture from Pacific storms; the west slopes receive large amounts of rain and snow, while the east slopes have a drier climate.

The Cascades are famous for their dense forests. Wet, cool conditions on the western slopes favor trees such as Douglas-fir, western redcedar, Pacific

Hiking the Todd Lake Trail below Broken Top.

silver fir, and mountain hemlock. Hotter, drier conditions on the eastern slopes favor ponderosa pine, lodgepole pine, Douglas-fir, grand fir, Engelmann spruce, and subalpine fir. Near timberline, where continuous forest gives way to tree islands and parklike alpine meadows, whitebark pine joins subalpine fir and mountain hemlock to form the subalpine forest.

Geographical relief is greater on the west side of the mountains than on the east. Many trails start below 3,000 feet on the west side, are longer, and have more vertical ascent. Most east side trails are 5,000 feet or higher in elevation.

GEOLOGY

The Cascades are young, active volcanic mountains. The recent eruption of Mount Saint Helens demonstrates that the volcanic action continues even today; recent ash fields and lava flows are common throughout the mountains. Other areas are heavily forested, but the luxurious growth barely conceals the volcanic underpinnings. Geologically speaking, the most recent volcanic activity is found in the high Cascades. The chain of lofty stratovolcanoes lined up along the crest of the range is dramatic proof. The lower, western mountains, sometimes called the Old Cascades, are also volcanic, but were formed during an older period of volcanic activity. Why do all these volcanoes erupt here? The answer lies deep within the Earth.

What we like to think of as solid land is actually a slab of rock about 25 miles thick, floating on the hot, semi-fluid rocks of the Earth's interior. The crust under the ocean floor is about 5.5 miles thick. These great slabs, or plates, of the Earth's crust are in very slow but constant motion. The Cascade Mountains mark the zone where the North American continental plate is colliding with the Pacific oceanic plate. The Pacific plate is diving beneath the North American plate and melting the underside of the continental plate as it descends. Some of the resulting super-hot, molten rock, called magma, finds its way upward through faults and other weaknesses in the crust. When the magma erupts into the air, it is called lava, cinders, or ash. The outpouring of lava and other volcanic rocks pile up to form mountains and plateaus.

CLIMATE

The Oregon Cascades have a dry summer season and a wet winter season. Most of the yearly rain and snowfall occurs from October through April. By late May the weather tends to dry out. Occasional thunderstorms do occur during late summer, but generally the weather remains dry until the first winter storms. These storms usually hit in mid-October but can occur as early as the first of September.

Typically, storms move in from the Pacific Ocean, continuing east over land. The low coast ranges intercept some of the moisture held in the clouds, but plenty remains when the moist air strikes the west side of the Cascades. As the wet air rises, it becomes more unstable and releases its moisture before crossing the crest of the mountains. As it descends the east slopes, the air becomes warmer and drier. On the west side of the mountains, winters tend to be wet and mild, while on the east side they are drier and colder.

The Cascades west of the crest receive 50 to 120 inches of moisture each year, which can include up to 500 inches of snowfall. As a result, the western slopes support the densest forest and have more streams and lakes. Precipitation is dramatically less on the east slopes. For instance, Santiam Pass, on the crest of the range, receives about 90 inches of precipitation per year. Sisters, just 20 miles to the east, receives only about 15 inches. This is why the east side forest is composed of trees such as ponderosa pine and lodgepole pine, which can tolerate the drier conditions. We see fewer brush and other understory plants and not as many lakes and streams.

The heavy snowpack may linger as late as early July at elevations of 6,000 feet or higher. Intermediate elevations are usually snow-free by May, and the west side hikes at 2,000 feet or lower are usually snow-free (but not rain-free!) all year. Insects, including mosquitoes, are most plentiful during the few weeks right after snow melt, a period that also brings the showiest flowers. Summer temperatures on the west side tend to range from 60 to 80 degrees Fahrenheit, although it can be warmer at lower elevations. Temperatures along the high crest typically range from 30 to 70 degrees. Along the eastern slopes, temperatures tend to range from 40 to 90 degrees.

As the forests and meadows dry out in August, flowers become less abundant. Occasional short periods of thunderstorm activity may produce heavy rain, but these storms are usually limited to small areas and last only a few hours. Some species of flowers linger into fall, when the hiking weather becomes ideal. Although the days are shorter and the nights chillier, autumn days in the Cascades are a delight thanks to the crisp, clear air.

EQUIPMENT

A modest amount of good equipment, along with the skill and technique to use it, make hiking safer and more enjoyable. Day hiking is popular because it can be enjoyed without a lot of time or specialized equipment. Often, beginners find they already have all the needed gear.

For many hikers, the step from day hiking to backpacking is a large one, and one that is often not taken. Somehow, the thought of sleeping out is daunting, as are the additional time, equipment, and skills required. However, the hiker who never stays out overnight is missing as much as the swimmer who only dangles his toes in the water. Start out easy by camping near a trailhead on a familiar trail, then gradually extend your range by camping farther from the road and staying out longer.

ESSENTIALS

On all hikes that are more than a casual stroll, you should carry certain essentials—water, food, rain/wind gear, sunglasses, sunscreen, knife, lighter or other reliable fire starter, map, compass, and flashlight. These items can easily be carried in a small fanny pack and may save your life if you are delayed or the weather changes.

Footwear

For short, easy hikes on good trails nearly any comfortable footwear, such as tennis shoes or running shoes, will work. Fit is very important—the shoe or boot should fit snugly but with plenty of toe room. To test for toe room, try the shoe on your largest foot wearing the socks you will hike in (see below). With the shoe still unlaced, stand up and slide your foot as far forward as it will go. You should be able to easily slip a finger behind your heel and wiggle it. If you have less room, your toes will hit the end of the shoe as you hike, causing pain and nasty blisters. Fit is especially important for children, since they can't determine the proper fit for themselves and won't complain until it is too late.

If you become a frequent hiker, you may want to buy a pair of light-weight hiking boots. These are suitable for longer, rougher trails. There are many models available in women's, men's, and children's sizes, constructed of nylon with leather reinforcing and molded rubber soles. Some of the more sophisticated and expensive designs use waterproof/breathable fabrics. Again, fit is the most important consideration.

For difficult hiking with heavy loads, some hikers prefer all-leather boots with soles that can be replaced when they wear out. Be careful not to buy the heavy, stiff boots intended for technical mountaineering. In fact, many of us prefer lightweight hiking boots even for very difficult cross-country hiking, trading durability for less weight on our feet.

Good quality, well-fitting socks are critical to hiking comfort. They provide not only insulation but also padding. A good combination is a light inner sock of cotton, wool, or polypropylene, with an outer medium- or heavyweight sock of wool with nylon reinforcing. The outer sock will tend to slide on the inner sock, rather than directly on your skin, reducing the chance of blisters. Inner socks of cotton are comfortable in warm weather, while polypropylene socks will wick moisture away from your skin in cool weather. Wool is still the best fiber for the outer cushioning sock, though a small percentage of nylon extends its life. A small amount of Spandex helps the sock keep its shape and fluffiness on long hikes.

Incipient blisters should be treated before they happen! At the first sign of a hot spot or other discomfort on your feet, stop and check it out. A hot spot can be protected with a piece of felt moleskin (available at drug stores—but since there aren't any drug stores in the backcountry, it's good to keep a few sheets in your first-aid kit). Often a change of socks will help as well. Once a blister has fully developed, it should be protected by a piece of moleskin with the center cut out around the raised area of skin, like a donut. A large or deep blister can be immobilizing, which is why prevention is so important.

Clothing

Nearly any durable clothing will do for hiking in good, stable weather. On hot, sunny days keep your skin covered with long sleeves and long pants or use a good sunscreen. In the mountains strong sun and high altitudes can produce painful sunburn in a short time, even on tanned skin; a brimmed sun hat is a good idea. Long pants will also protect your skin from scratches when hiking a brushy trail.

Give a little more thought to your clothing in cool, windy, or changeable weather; several layers of light, flexible clothing work better than single heavy, cumbersome layers, such as winter parkas. Down is the lightest, most durable insulation, but it's hard to dry when wet. When you expect wet weather, consider a jacket insulated with a synthetic fill. Synthetic pile or fleece, which is marketed under a bewildering variety of trade names, is the warmest, driest insulator for very wet conditions. Even when soaked it can be wrung out and worn immediately.

In cool weather, a warm wool or synthetic watch cap or balaclava makes an amazing difference in comfort—up to half your body's heat is lost through your head. Protect your hands with wool or synthetic gloves or mittens.

The layer system becomes even more important while backpacking because you'll want to keep your load as light as possible. It's easy to select clothes for mild, stable weather, but when storms threaten take more care. Make certain that you have at least one good layer of insulation, such as a down or synthetic pile jacket, and bring a set of good quality rain gear. In cold, wet weather, the four layer system works well—the inner layer consists of lightweight, synthetic, wicking long underwear; the next layer consists of sturdy pants and a sturdy shirt that will stand up to brush and rocks; the third layer consists of an insulating jacket or parka. The fourth layer consists of a good set of rain pants and jacket with hood. If this outer layer is constructed from a waterproof and breathable fabric, then it will do double duty as a wind shell.

Don't put up with being overheated or chilled. Stop to add or subtract layers as necessary to stay comfortable.

Food

You should bring some food on all but the shortest hikes. High calorie food keeps your energy levels high. You can make sandwiches and other picnic items or bring fruit, cheese, crackers, nuts, and drink mixes. I like to keep an athletic energy bar or two in my pack so I always have something to eat, even if I don't take anything else.

Although a great deal of dehydrated food is made especially for backpacking and lightweight camping, it tends to be very expensive. Many items found in supermarkets make good backpacking food at lower cost. Using just supermarket food, I have been able to do many backpack trips with no more than 1.75 pounds of food per person per day. Some suggestions for breakfast include low bulk cold cereals with powdered milk, hot cereals,

6

dried fruit, breakfast bars, hot chocolate, tea, and coffee. For lunch take munchies such as nuts, cheese, crackers, dried fruit, candy bars, athletic energy bars, dried soup, hard candy, beef or turkey jerky, sardines, and fruit-flavored drink mixes. For dinner try dried noodle or rice-based dishes supplemented with margarine and a small can of tuna, turkey, or chicken.

Before leaving home, remove excess packaging from the food items to reduce weight. Plastic bags with zipper closures make excellent food re-packaging bags. Messy items should be double bagged. Pack margarine and peanut butter in reliable, wide mouth plastic jars (available from outdoor suppliers). Unless you really trust the seal, put the container in a plastic bag also! Extra bags are useful during the trip for double bagging messy trash such as sardine cans.

Water

Water is the most important item in your pack, especially during hot weather. On day hikes, bring water from home. Even in wet country, you should bring a quart of water. Some of the hikes in this book do not have any reliable water sources during the dry season, so be sure you have enough. Each hiker may drink a gallon or more during a long, difficult hike.

On backpack trips, you will have to use water from wilderness springs, streams, or lakes. Always purify it with a reliable water purification system.

The best water containers are plastic bottles with leak-proof caps, carried inside your pack. Another popular arrangement is a fanny pack with external bottle carriers. Metal canteens carried on your belt or on a shoulder strap are uncomfortable and the water is heated by the sun.

Knife

A knife is necessary for many routine tasks, such as cutting cord, and is vital for emergency fire building. Personal preference will dictate what type of knife you'll want to carry. Some hikers prefer the Swiss Army type with scissors and other implements, while others like a simple, large-bladed knife such as a folding hunter.

Sunglasses

A good pair of sunglasses is essential when traveling in open areas during the summer. Good glasses are optically correct and remove invisible ultra-violet and infrared light, reducing eyestrain and headaches. Ultraviolet protection is especially important at high altitude and on summer snowfields. The tag on the glasses will specify whether ultraviolet or infrared light is filtered. Cheap sunglasses with no ultraviolet protection are worse than no sunglasses—they reduce visible light, causing the iris to open and admit more damaging ultraviolet rays. Excessive ultraviolet exposure causes snow blindness, a temporary but very uncomfortable condition. Hikers who are dependent on prescription glasses or contact lenses should carry a spare pair of glasses in a hard plastic case for protection.

Sunscreen

Sunscreen is another essential item. Lotions are rated by their Sun Protection Factor, or SPF, which approximates the length of time you are protected as compared to unprotected skin. For example, a sunscreen rated at SPF 15 gives about fifteen times your natural protection. Theoretically, you can stay in the sun fifteen times longer than if you wore no sunscreen. A wide range of SPF values are available; err on the side of caution. Few things can ruin a backpack trip more completely than a bad sunburn. Remember that the sun is much more intense on summer snowfields than deep in a forest.

Pack

A well-fitting, well-made day pack goes a long way toward making your hike a pleasant experience. Good packs are not cheap, but they will last a long time. Look for firm foam padding on the back panel and on the shoulder straps. Larger day packs usually have a waist belt, which may or may not be padded, and a reinforced bottom. Fanny packs are another popular alternative. They are especially nice in warm weather because they allow your back to have free air circulation. Their main drawback is limited holding capacity, which makes them unsuited for long hikes in remote areas or in changing weather. Fanny packs work well for young children, because they can carry a token amount of gear and feel included in the group.

Packs for backpacking fall into two categories, internal frame and external frame. Internal frame packs have the frame built into the pack; the pack rides closer to your body and balances well for cross-country hiking. External frame packs are usually made of aluminum tubing with a separately attached packbag. They are easier to pack and to overload, for extended trips. They also give better back ventilation in hot weather.

A good backpack of either type carefully distributes the load between your shoulders, back, and hips, with most of the weight on your hips, so correct fit is critical. The best place to buy a pack is from an outdoor store that is staffed by hikers knowledgeable in pack fitting. If you buy a pack by mail order, get the advice of an experienced friend and make certain you can return it unused if necessary. Check the fit carefully before using it in the field. Be cautious when buying a used pack. A poor fit negates any monetary savings. Women should be careful when thinking of buying or borrowing a pack from a male friend. Because of women's lesser average height and shorter torso, it is rare for a man's pack to fit well. Most pack manufacturers make packs designed specifically for women.

There are also overnight packs designed for children. Introduce your children to short day hikes at an early age, gradually lengthening the distance as they grow older and their stamina and interest increase. Their first overnight hikes can be kept short, as they should be for any novice hiker, child or adult. Once a child is old enough to carry a pack, keep its load light. If you progressively introduce your children to backpacking, by the time they are energetic teenagers they'll be addicted to hiking. You may even persuade them to carry some of your own load. (In your dreams!)

A loaded pack means that you'll walk at a slower pace, especially uphill. Remember to allow for this when planning overnight trips versus day hikes. Walking sticks are helpful, especially at stream crossings or other places where the footing is uncertain. They can also be used to push brush and low branches out of the way, as a prop to turn a pack into a back rest, or to support a tarp for shelter.

Sleeping Bag

Your sleeping bag is one of the most important items in your pack. With a good one you'll most likely have a comfortable sleep; a poor bag will guarantee a miserable experience. The manufacturer's warranty is a good indicator of quality. A well-made sleeping bag should have a lifetime warranty against defects, while a cheaper one may only be guaranteed for only a year. The occasional user may be happy with a backpacker-style mummy bag insulated with one of the current synthetic fills. Synthetic fills have the advantages of lower initial cost and of retaining some of their insulating ability when soaking wet. High-quality down fill, though expensive, is still unsurpassed in insulating capability for its weight. Since it is more durable, down is actually less expensive than synthetics over the lifetime of the bag. People who backpack often tend to prefer down bags. Down is also more water resistant than commonly thought, as anyone who has tried to wash a down bag by hand can tell you. Sleeping bags are rated by temperature and sometimes by recommended seasons. A three-season bag is adequate for most backpacking. If you sleep warm, you may wish to get a lighter bag, and if you sleep cold, you'll probably prefer a warmer bag.

Sleeping Pad

Since lightweight sleeping bags don't provide much insulation or padding underneath, you'll need a sleeping pad. The best type currently available is the self-inflating, foam-filled air mattress. These are less prone to punctures than a traditional air mattress, are much warmer, and at least as comfortable. Closed-cell foam pads are a cheaper alternative. They insulate very well but are not especially comfortable. A compromise is the open-cell foam pad. Since the porous cells absorb water just like a sponge, these pads have a waterproof cover. Open-cell pads are comfortable but heavy and bulky to carry.

Shelter

Most hikers depend on a tent for shelter. Sound construction and high quality are important. A three-season, two-man dome or free-standing tent is the most versatile. Larger tents are more awkward to carry and require more spacious campsites. Nearly all tents use a separate waterproof fly over the tent canopy, which provides rain protection and also allows moisture to escape from within the tent. Small children can share a tent with their parents, but as they get older, kids often enjoy their own.

Some experienced hikers avoid the weight and expense of a tent by carrying a tarp with a separate groundsheet. A tarp provides good weather protection if set up properly and is versatile enough to use as a sun shade or wind break during lunch stops. Using a tarp effectively does take some practice. Also, a tarp provides no protection from mosquitoes and other insects!

Avoid plastic tube tents. In the store, they look simple and attractive, but in the field they're a nightmare. The plastic condenses moisture from your body that then collects on the walls and runs down under your sleeping bag. It's nearly impossible to close the open ends against wind-driven rain and, even if successful, it just makes the condensation problem worse.

First-aid Kit

A small first-aid kit will do for day hikes, but you'll definitely need a more complete kit for backpacking. Make sure that you get one intended specifically for wilderness sports. Judging by the sales rate, I suspect that most hikers don't bother with a kit. That's unfortunate, because minor problems such as cuts, scrapes, and blisters can easily become serious without treatment.

Accessories

A camera is probably the most common "extra" item carried on day hikes. Consider bringing a nylon ditty bag or plastic bag to protect it if rain is a possibility. Even the most waterproof packs can leak through seams and zippers. This advice also applies to any other items in your pack that could be damaged by water, such as maps.

EQUIPMENT SOURCES

Local outdoors shops staffed by people who use the gear and are willing to share their knowledge with you are valuable resources worth supporting. If you can't find a good local shop, then look into mail order. There are several reputable companies—check ads in outdoor recreation magazines for addresses and phone numbers.

MAKING IT A SAFE TRIP

Wilderness can be a safe place, if you are willing to respect your limitations. Once you develop confidence in your technique and equipment, then you will become at ease in the backcountry. Hikers should be self reliant; this capability can be safely developed by starting out with easy hikes and progressing to more difficult adventures as your experience broadens.

Moraine Lake reflects South Sister.

Many wilderness accidents are caused by individuals or parties pushing too hard. Instead, set reasonable goals, allowing for delays caused by weather, deteriorated trails, slow members of your party, unexpectedly rough country, and dry springs. Be flexible enough to eliminate part of a hike if your original plans appear too ambitious. Do not fall into the trap of considering a trip plan "cast in stone." Rather, take pride in your adaptability.

With experience, operating in the backcountry becomes a welcome relief from the complex tangle of civilized living. Wilderness decisions are usually important but also basic in nature. While "out there," things that seemed important in civilization lose some of their urgency. In other words, we gain a sense of perspective.

TRIP PLANNING

Maps are essential for trip planning and should be obtained in advance. Guidebooks allow you to learn about an area more quickly than you could with maps alone. Once you are comfortable with an area and have done many of the hikes in the guidebooks, you will be able to plan your own hikes using maps and information from other hikers to help you.

When planning a backpacking trip, consider alternatives to traditional campsites. Dry camping, or camping with just the water you carry, is a valuable skill with many advantages. Dry camping virtually eliminates the possibility of contaminating wilderness streams and lakes. You can avoid heavily used campsites and their camp-robbing animal attendants, such as skunks, mice, gray jays, and insects. Dry camping opens up many beautiful, uncrowded campsites. The technique is simple. Use a collapsible water container to pick up water at the last reliable source of the day, then use minimum water for camp chores. Plan your route so that you pass a reliable water source each day of the trip or, better, late in the afternoon and again first thing in the morning.

WATER ESSENTIALS

Backcountry water sources are not safe to drink. Appearance is no indication of safety—even sparkling clear water may contain harmful parasites. Contamination comes from wild and domestic animals as well as increasing human use. Infections from contaminated water are uncomfortable and can be disabling. Giardiasis, for example, is a severe gastrointestinal infection caused by small cysts; it can require an emergency evacuation of the infected hiker. Giardiasis is spread by all mammals, including humans.

Purify all water sources unless you are positive that they are safe. Iodine tablets, available from outdoors shops, are the most effective wilderness water purification system. (See *Medicine for Mountaineering* in Appendix B.) One iodine tablet per quart will kill nearly all dangerous organisms, including *giardia* cysts. Carefully read and follow the directions on the bottle to ensure effective use. In order to retain their potency, the tablets must be kept dry until used, and it's a good idea to discard opened bottles after a trip. For those who find the iodine taste objectionable an iodine taste remover tablet is now available that restores the original color and taste of the water without altering the iodine's effectiveness. Since the active biocidal agent is removed by these tablets, make sure you wait until the iodine tablets have had time to purify the water before adding these remover tablets. Fruit and sport drinks containing ascorbic acid (vitamin C) have the same effect. Some people use such drink mixes to mask the taste of the iodine. If you do so, wait until the tablets have done their work before adding the drink mix

Water filters are a popular alternative to iodine treatment, largely due to the better-tasting water they produce. But they are quite a bit heavier to carry than iodine tablets and also take longer to use. Filters cannot remove viruses (that are smaller than the pores in the filter elements), but some use active iodine elements to kill viruses.

Water can also be purified by bringing it to a rolling boil. It's not necessary to continue heating the water past this point. Boiling is effective at any altitude, but has the main drawbacks that it uses extra fuel and gives the water a flat taste. The latter problem is easily fixed by pouring the water back and forth between two containers several times. This restores the dissolved air that boiling removes.

Chlorine tablets and household bleach are not reliable for wilderness water purification. Small amounts of organic matter combine with the purifying agent to reduce its effectiveness. Also, chlorine tablets rapidly lose their strength once the bottle is opened and the tablets are exposed to air.

BACKCOUNTRY NAVIGATION

Maps

Several different types of maps are available for wilderness navigation. Topographic maps are the most useful because they show the elevation and shape of the land through the use of contour lines. All of the Oregon Cascades are covered by the 7.5-minute quadrangle series published by the U.S. Geological Survey. Each hike description in this book lists the USGS topographic maps that cover the hike. The USGS maps are produced from aerial photos to high standards of accuracy. At a scale of 1:24,000 (2.6 inches to the mile) and printed in sheets that cover about 7 by 9 miles, these are usually the most detailed maps available. The only catch is that the USGS can't update the maps very often, so manmade details such as trails and roads may be out of date. USGS maps are sometimes sold in outdoors shops and engineering supply stores. Check the local Yellow Pages under "maps." USGS maps are also available by mail order from the USGS map distribution center in Denver. See the list of resources in Appendix A for the current address. Request a free state index and catalog of the topographic maps.

The Forest Service and several private companies publish topographic maps of the wilderness areas covered in this book. Although these maps have limited coverage outside the designated wilderness areas, trail and road information is usually more up-to-date. Scales vary from 1:63,360 to 1:24,000 (1 to 2.6 inches per mile). If a wilderness map for a hike in this book is available, it is listed under "maps." Wilderness maps are available from the ranger stations and offices listed in Appendix A and from outdoor shops and bookstores.

Planimetric maps can also be useful. These maps are essentially road maps because they don't have contour lines. The Forest Service publishes a useful series of planimetric maps that cover the national forests. These maps show the forest road system at a scale of 1:126,720 (0.5 inch to the mile). They also include the official road numbers that are shown on road signs, which makes the forest maps most valuable for locating a trailhead. The relevant national forest map is listed for each hike in the book. Some Forest Service offices also have topographic forest maps at various scales and coverages. Forest Service maps are available from the ranger stations and offices listed in Appendix A, as well as outdoors shops and bookstores.

Map reading is a skill that requires practice, but it pays off in increased safety in the backcountry. The best way to learn is to get a map of an area that you already know. Go to a place with an overview of the terrain and spend some time relating what you see to the map symbols. It will be easier at first if you orient the map with the terrain. To do this, turn the map until map north and true north are aligned. As you gain experience, you'll be able to relate the map to ground features even without orienting it. Use the legend or symbol key to learn the map symbols and compare them to the actual terrain features. (To save space, most USGS maps don't have a symbol key printed on the map itself. You can obtain one from the USGS or a map dealer.)

The most important symbols on topographic maps are the brown contour lines. Each line represents a constant elevation above sea level. For example, if sea level rose to 4,000 feet, then the 4,000-foot contour would become the new shoreline. Contour lines are spaced at regular intervals specified on the map—usually 40 vertical feet in the mountains. To make them easier to read, every fourth or fifth contour is printed darker for emphasis. These index contours also have the elevation in feet printed along the line. Contour lines spread out on gentle slopes and bunch up on steep slopes. Ridges show up as a series of V-shaped contours; drainages look similar but may have a blue line representing the streambed running through the apex of the Vs. With a little practice, you'll be able to visualize the terrain in three dimensions just from scanning the map.

Before entering the backcountry, study the maps to become familiar with the general lay of the land. This is a good time to establish a baseline—a long, unmistakable landmark, such as a road or highway, that borders the area. In the rare event that you become totally disoriented, you can always use your compass to follow a general course toward your baseline as a last resort.

Trail signs may be vandalized or inaccurate. It is better to stay aware of your location at all times and use the trail signs as confirmation. While hiking, refer to the map often and locate yourself in reference to visible landmarks. If you do this consistently, without relying on trail signs, you will never become lost.

Compasses

Always carry a reliable, liquid-filled compass so that you can determine directions in dense forest or bad weather. Because backcountry navigation consists primarily of map reading, your compass will probably languish in your pack for years before you use it! When you finally do need it, you will need it badly—not a good time to find out that the needle has fallen off.

Good compasses come with instructions. Refer to these for details on using your particular brand and model. There are several good books on compass work and orienteering. A word of caution though—classic orienteering techniques emphasize travel in straight lines along compass courses, which is not usually practical in the mountains.

Global Positioning System

The satellite navigation system maintained by the Department of Defense makes it possible to find your location nearly anywhere on Earth. GPS consists of a set of twenty-four satellites orbiting 12,000 miles above the Earth. Low-cost, portable receivers are available, which are designed specifically for ground navigation. The readout shows your position within about 330 feet (100 meters). Weather conditions do not affect the accuracy of GPS, but the receiver must have a clear view of the sky. This means that dense forest, narrow canyons, or poor satellite geometry can prevent an accurate fix. If this happens, move to another location or wait a few minutes before trying again.

A GPS unit is no substitute for a good map and a reliable compass. In fact, the coordinates shown on the GPS readout are not even very useful without a map. Still, there are times and places when a GPS receiver can be extremely valuable. Keep in mind that the GPS unit is useless if the batteries die. Take spares! Also be aware that the receiver can take a few minutes to reach its best accuracy. Instead of using the receiver while on the move, take a reading at rest stops. This not only gives better accuracy, but also saves time and batteries. With a clear view of the sky and good satellite geometry, the position shown changes slowly over a range of about 330 feet (100 meters). Once the displayed position is consistently within this distance, then reading is accurate. GPS receivers remember the position of the satellites in the sky and produce an accurate reading more quickly if they have been used recently.

When buying a unit for hiking, make sure it uses the UTM coordinate system as well as latitude and longitude. UTM is found on USGS topographic maps and is easier to use than the latitude and longitude system. Any map accurate enough for wilderness navigation will at least have the latitude and longitude coordinate system.

TRAIL COURTESY

Never cut switchbacks on trails. Shortcutting actually takes more physical effort than staying on the trail. It also increases erosion and the need for trail maintenance. Give horses and other pack animals the right of way by stepping off the trail downhill. Talk in a normal tone of voice and don't make sudden movements or loud noises, which can spook an animal.

You will probably encounter mountain bikes outside designated wilderness areas. Since they're less maneuverable than you, it's polite to step aside so the riders can pass without having to veer off the trail.

Smokers should stop at a bare spot or rock ledge, then make certain that all smoking materials are out before continuing. Never smoke or light any kind of fire on windy days or when the fire danger is high, because wildfires will start easily and spread explosively.

Although dogs are allowed in national forests and designated wilderness areas, they are best left at home. Barking dogs disturb other hikers, and their presence places unnecessary stress on beleaguered wildlife. If you do bring your dog, either keep it on a leash or under voice command at all times. Dogs are not allowed on trails in national parks and monuments.

There are too many of us in the backcountry now to support outdated practices such as cutting live trees or plants of any kind, blazing or carving initials on trees or rocks, picking wildflowers, and building rock campfire rings.

Never disturb ruins or other old sites and artifacts. These sites are protected by the Antiquities Act, which is intended to preserve our historic and prehistoric heritage. Archaeologists study artifacts in place because the setting reveals more information than the artifact alone. Once a site is disturbed, another piece of the puzzle is gone forever.

Motorized vehicles and bicycles, including mountain bikes, are prohibited in all designated wilderness areas. State parks and other areas also may have restrictions.

CAMPING

Start looking for a campsite at least a couple of hours before dark. Campsites become harder to find as the group size increases—a good reason to avoid groups larger than five or six people. The best camps are on reasonably level sites with dry, sandy soil, bare rock, or forest duff. Avoid fragile, easily damaged sites like grassy meadows, lakeshores, and stream banks. Select a site that's screened from trails, meadows, and other campsites. As a rule of thumb, camp out of sight and sound of others; respect their desire for wilderness solitude. Land managers sometimes close specific areas to camping or entry to allow it to recover from heavy use. If such restrictions are in place, follow them. In the hike descriptions, I describe restrictions in effect at the time of writing. These regulations change from year to year as sites are rehabilitated. Check with the office listed under each hike before planning your trip. Also, information brochures are often available at trailheads.

If bad weather threatens, look for a campsite sheltered from wind and blowing rain, preferably with natural drainage and an absorbent surface, such as forest duff or sand. Heavy forest provides protection from rain at the beginning of a storm, but the trees drip for hours after the rain stops. Never dig drainage ditches or excavate dirt to level a campsite; these practices cause erosion and severe damage. A slight slope will keep groundwater from pooling under your tent. Modern sleeping pads make it possible to camp on gravel or even rock slabs in comfort. During hot weather, look for shade, especially from the morning sun. In heavy forest, check overhead for "widowmakers," large, dead branches that may break off and crash down.

CAMPFIRES

Although many hikers enjoy the freedom and convenience of cooking meals on a backpacker's stove, for others a campfire is an essential part of the camping experience. To enjoy a campfire responsibly, use an established campfire ring if available, otherwise look for a site in gravel, sand, or bare soil. The ground should be naturally bare around your fire site to prevent the fire from spreading. Then dig a shallow pit, heaping dirt around the edges to form a wind and fire break. Do not use stones, because they become permanently blackened. Pick up dead wood from the ground or break dead limbs from trees. There's no need to carry a saw or an ax. If you need such implements to collect wood, then it's too scarce to justify building a campfire except in an emergency. Keep your fire small to conserve wood and minimize ashes. Large fires escape more easily and have a nasty tendency to throw sparks on your expensive equipment.

Backpacker's trash is so light it can be easily carried out. Don't try to burn it. Many paper packages are lined with aluminum foil that does not burn in any campfire, no matter how hot. Plastic also does not burn well and may give off highly toxic fumes. Unfortunately, there are plenty of old fire pits full of charred plastic and sparkling bits of aluminum to prove the point.

When ready to leave camp, first make sure your campfire is cold by adding water or dirt to the coals and stirring until there is no visible smoke or heat. Then, check the ashes with your bare hand. Finally, cover the fire pit with the dirt saved from the original pit and scatter any remaining wood. After a short time, your fire site will look natural again.

Campfires should never be built where prohibited by regulation, in heavily used areas, or near timberline where wood is scarce. All fires may be prohibited by land managers when the fire danger is high. Never build a fire on a windy day even during low fire danger. Check the trailhead bulletin board for current information on campfire restrictions.

TRASH

If you carried it in, you can also carry it out. Lightweight food that has been carefully repacked to eliminate excess packaging produces little trash even after a week or more in the backcountry. Avoid burying food or trash, because after you leave animals will find it by smell, dig it up, and scatter it all over the place. Don't feed wild creatures, since they will become dependent on human food, which is not good for them and can lead to their starvation during the winter.

SANITATION

Wilderness sanitation is the most critical skill we need to practice to keep the backcountry pristine. A short walk in any popular recreation area will show that few people seem to know how to relieve themselves when pit toilets are not available. Naturally occurring diseases, such as giardiasis, are aggravated by poor human sanitation. Fortunately wilderness sanitation is mostly common sense. If facilities are available, use them! Their presence means that the human population of the area is too large for the natural disposal systems of the soil. In the backcountry, select a site at least 100 yards from streams, lakes, springs, and dry washes, avoiding barren, sandy soil if possible. Next, dig a small "cat-hole" about 6 inches into the organic layer of the soil. (Some people carry a small plastic trowel for this purpose.) When finished, refill the hole, covering any toilet paper.

FIRST AID

At least one member of the party should have current first-aid skills. *Medicine for Mountaineering* (see Appendix B) and several other books are excellent sources of wilderness medical information.

WEATHER

During the summer, heat can be a hazard on the eastern slopes and at lower elevations. In hot weather, a gallon or more of water will be needed by each hiker every day. To avoid dehydration, drink more water than required merely to quench your thirst. Sport drinks, which replace electrolytes, are also useful.

Protection both from the heat and the sun is important. A lightweight sun hat is an essential. During hot weather, plan hikes at higher elevations or hike early in the day to avoid the afternoon heat. Summer backpack trips can be planned to take advantage of the long days by hiking from first light to midmorning, taking a long, shady lunch break, then finishing the day's walk in early evening when it cools off.

If towering cumulus clouds appear, presaging a thunderstorm and its deadly lightning, get off exposed ridges and mountain tops and stay away from lone trees.

Avoid continuous exposure to chilling weather, which may subtly lower body temperature and cause sudden collapse from hypothermia, a life-threatening condition. Cool winds, especially with rain, are the most dangerous because the heat loss is insidious. Hypothermia may be completely prevented by wearing enough layers of clothing to avoid chilling and by eating and drinking regularly so that your body produces heat. Snow may fall at any time of year on the higher mountains. Be prepared for it by bringing more layers of warm clothing than you think you will need. During the wet season, use synthetic garments made of polypropylene or polyester fibers, because these fibers retain their insulating ability when wet better than any natural fiber, including wool.

INSECTS AND THEIR KIN

Mosquitoes appear right after snowmelt and persist for a month or so. Late summer and early fall are the best times for avoiding them. A good insect repellent is essential on all hikes, and most backpackers prefer to carry a tent that has fine ("no-see-um") netting on the doors and windows.

Scorpions are found nearly everywhere in Oregon, but the species found here are not hazardous. The stings are no more painful than a bee sting.

Other insects such as bees and wasps, also give non-threatening but painful stings. One exception is for people who have a known allergic reaction to specific insect stings. Since this reaction can develop rapidly and be life-threatening, such people should check with their doctor to see if desensitization treatment is recommended. They should also carry insect sting kits prescribed by their doctors.

SNAKES

Rattlesnakes are not common at the higher elevations, but may be encountered in lower, warmer country. They can easily be avoided because they usually warn intruders by rattling well before striking range. Never handle or tease any snake. Since rattlesnakes can strike a distance of approximately half their body length, avoid placing your hands and feet in areas that you cannot see, and walk several feet away from rock overhangs and shady ledges. Bites usually occur on the feet or ankles, so ankle-high hiking boots and loose fitting long pants will prevent most injuries. Snakes prefer surfaces with a temperature of about 80 degrees F. during hotter weather, and prefer the shade of bushes or rock overhangs. In cooler weather they will be found on open ground.

WILDLIFE

Wild animals normally leave you alone unless molested or provoked. Black bears are shy and not usually a problem; grizzlies are not found in Oregon. Once again, don't ever feed any wild animal, since they rapidly get used to handouts and will vigorously defend their new food source. Around camp, problems with rodents can be avoided by hanging your food from rocks or trees. Even the toughest pack can be wrecked by a determined mouse or squirrel that has all night to work. Needless to say, heavily used campsites present the worst problems.

PLANTS

The leaves and stems of poison oak and poison ivy are harmful to the touch. Both are easily recognized by their leaves, which grow in groups of three. Contact with either of these plants causes a rash that can later blister. Unless large areas of skin are involved or the reaction is severe, no specific treatment is required. Calamine lotion will relieve the itching.

Never eat any plant unless you can positively identify it. Many common plants, especially mushrooms, are deadly.

RESCUE

Anyone entering remote country should be self-sufficient and prepared to take care of emergencies such as equipment failure and minor medical problems. Very rarely, circumstances may create a life-threatening situation that requires an emergency evacuation or a search effort. Always leave word of your hiking plans with a reliable individual. For backpack trips, you should provide a written itinerary. The responsible person should be advised to contact the appropriate authority if you fail to return when you say you will. In your instructions, allow extra time for routine delays. In the area covered by this book, the authority responsible for search and rescue is the county sheriff. Phone numbers are available at the front of most phone books. The Forest Service cooperates with the sheriff's department and may also be contacted in the event of an emergency.

Don't count on a cellular phone for communications in the backcountry. The cellular phone system is dependent on a closely spaced network of short-range radio transmitters designed for use in cities and populated areas. Cell phone coverage is not continuous in rural areas and may be nonexistent in wilderness. Even if you can alert authorities to your problem, you will have a better chance of surviving until rescuers arrive if you are self-sufficient.

AUTHOR'S RECOMMENDATIONS

EASY DAY HIKES

Hike 1 (Pansy Lake), Hike 7 (Firecamp Lakes), Hike 10 (South Breitenbush Gorge), Hike 13 (Marion Lake), Hike 20 (Wasco Lake), Hike 21 (Square Lake), Hike 29 (Clear Lake), Hike 30 (Waterfalls Trail), Hike 33 (Hand Lake), Hike 41 (Olallie Trail), Hike 55 (Koch Mountain Trail), Hike 59 (Waldo Lake Shoreline Trail), Hike 60 (Betty Lake), Hike 64 (Hemlock Butte), Hike 66 (Rosary Lakes), and Hike 67 (Eagle Rock).

VERY EASY DAY HIKES FOR PARENTS WITH SMALL CHILDREN

Hike 23 (Metolius River), Hike 26 (Hackleman Creek Old-Growth Trail), Hike 29 (Clear Lake), Hike 38 (Proxy Falls), Hike 39 (Linton Lake), Hike 43 (French Pete Creek), Hike 44 (Rebel Creek), Hike 50 (Fall Creek), Hike 46 (Little Three Creek Lake), Hike 67 (Eagle Rock), Hike 71 (Summit Lake), and Hike 72 (Pacific Crest National Scenic Trail).

FIRST NIGHT IN THE WILDERNESS

Hike 17 (Carl Lake) and Hike 63 (Divide Lake).

LONG DAY HIKES

Hike 6 (Park Ridge), Hike 9 (Jefferson Park), Hike 12 (Whitewater Trail), Hike 15 (Santiam Lake), Hike 24 (Trout Creek Trail), Hike 28 (Patjens Lakes), Hike 45 (Erma Bell Lakes), Hike 52 (Sisters Mirror Lake), Hike 54 (Paulina Lake), Hike 56 (Klovdahl Bay), Hike 68 (Hidden Lake), and Hike 69 (Yoran Lake).

HIKES FOR PHOTOGRAPHERS

Hike 9 (Jefferson Park), Hike 18 (Rockpile Lake), Hike 19 (Canyon Creek Meadows), Hike 29 (Clear Lake), Hike 30 (Waterfalls Trail), Hike 48 (Broken Top Trail), Hike 61 (Diamond Falls), and Hike 63 (Divide Lake).

HIKES WITH LOTS OF SIDE TRIPS AND EXPLORING

Hike 9 (Jefferson Park), Hike 37 (Three Sisters), Hike 49 (Todd Lake Trail), Hike 51 (Wickiup Plain), and Hike 58 (Rigdon Lake Loop).

BARRIER-FREE TRAILS

Hike 26 (Hackleman Creek Old-Growth Trail), Hike 45 (Erma Bell Lakes to Lower Erma Bell Lake), and Hike 61 (Diamond Falls first section).

HIKES FOR PEAK BAGGERS

Hike 2 (Bull of the Woods Trail), Hike 3 (Olallie Butte), Hike 8 (Bear Point), Hike 11 (Triangulation Peak), Hike 14 (Coffin Mountain), Hike 16 (Maxwell Butte), Hike 22 (Black Butte), Hike 35 (Black Crater), Hike 40 (Castle Rock), Hike 42 (Olallie Mountain), Hike 53 (Cinder Hill), Hike 57 (Fuji Mountain), Hike 64 (Hemlock Butte), Hike 65 (Maiden Peak), and Hike 75 (Tipsoo Peak).

HIKES FOR BACKPACKERS

Hike 9 (Jefferson Park), Hike 12 (Whitewater Trail), Hike 37 (Three Sisters), Hike 45 (Erma Bell Lakes), Hike 48 (Broken Top Trail), Hike 49 (Todd Lake Trail), and Hike 56 (Klovdahl Bay).

USING THIS GUIDE

The hikes are grouped in sections based on the major wilderness areas. Trails both inside and outside the base wilderness are included. Generally, the hikes are described from north to south, starting on the western slopes and moving to the eastern slopes, in each section.

Following each section, I've listed some additional trails. These are hikes that may be of interest but aren't covered in detail.

A map shows each hike, with emphasis on major landmarks, trail junctions, and the trailhead and destination. An elevation profile shows the general pattern of elevation gain and loss for the hike. For one-way, round-trip hikes, the profile shows only the outbound trip. Loop hikes and hikes that are a combination of one-way sections and loop sections are shown entirely. The scales vary on the maps and elevation profiles; check carefully when comparing hikes.

GENERAL DESCRIPTION

This lists the type of hike (day hike or backpack trip), special attractions, and the name of the designated wilderness or other special area, if any.

GENERAL LOCATION

Approximate road miles and directions are given from the nearest major town with basic tourist services, such as gasoline and groceries.

MAPS

Here, maps are listed that are useful for finding the trailhead and doing the hike. The appropriate U.S. Geological Survey, 7.5-minute topographic maps and the Forest Service map are always listed. The wilderness map is listed if available for the area.

DIFFICULTY

All the hikes are rated as easy, moderate, or difficult. An easy hike is generally less than 5 miles total length, has less than 500 feet elevation gain, and follows a well-maintained, marked trail. Nearly anyone should be able to do these hikes. Moderate hikes generally are between 5 and 10 miles total length, may have up to 2,000 feet elevation gain, and follow good trails. Most hikers will be able to do the moderate hikes; be prepared to spend part or all of the day.

Hikes rated as difficult involve more than 10 miles total distance or more than 2,000 feet elevation gain. A difficult hike may have cross-country travel or sections on unmaintained or unmarked trails. These hikes may require most of the day and should be attempted only by experienced hikers who are aware of their fitness level. Backpack trips take two or more days; the time required depends on the speed of the group and its objectives. Please be aware that the perceived difficulty of a hike varies with the individual hiker, load carried, season, and amount of trail maintenance.

LENGTH

This is the total distance of the hike in miles. That distance may be traveled round-trip or as a loop hike. Since trail distances are difficult to measure

Fall Creek.

precisely in the field, I place more emphasis on landmarks to locate important features, such as trail junctions, water sources, and campsites. Trail signs are usually noted if they were present when I last did the hike, but don't rely on any sign still being in place!

ELEVATION

Listed are the minimum and maximum elevation, in feet, that will be encountered on the hike. The lowest and highest elevations do not necessarily occur at the ends of the trail. If the hike is a descent (into a canyon, for example) that requires a climb on the return, then the highest elevation is listed first. Keep in mind that some of the hikes are at elevations of 5,000 feet or more, and the thin air may affect your hiking ability. Refer to each hike's elevation profile for a general look at the ups and downs along the route.

BEST SEASON

This is the recommended time of year to do the hike. In unusual years, the hiking season may be longer or shorter than indicated. Hikes that are noted as "year-round" may be hot during midsummer, so be certain to carry enough water.

FOR MORE INFORMATION

You can contact the government office listed here for up-to-date information, such as snowpack and trail conditions. Refer to Appendix A for the complete address and phone number.

HIKING PERMITS

As of this writing, hiking permits are required for all day hikes and backpack trips in all the designated wilderness areas covered in this book. This includes the Bull of the Woods, Diamond Peak, Menagerie, Mount Jefferson, Mount Thielsen, Mount Washington, Three Sisters, and Waldo Lake wilderness areas. In most cases the permit is self-issued at the trailhead, where a bulletin board gives the latest information and regulations for the area. Certain heavily used places and trailheads have been designated as limited entry areas. Permits for limited entry areas *must be obtained in advance at the specified ranger station.*

Most hikes outside of the designated wilderness do not currently require permits, but this may change in the future. Bulletin boards at the trailhead may post notices requesting you to fill out a voluntary registration form. This information is used to track backcountry use levels. It's a good idea to register, because the Forest Service uses the information to justify more funding for trail maintenance and protection of the area.

You should be aware that trailhead registration, whether voluntary or required, does not substitute for leaving a copy of your trip plans with a responsible individual. The Forest Service does not keep track of individual parties and cannot know if a group is overdue.

The Forest Service is considering a trailhead parking fee system, which may be in place by the time this book is published. It will probably work the same way as the present winter Sno-Park system, where a parking permit must be bought in advance, then displayed on the vehicle while parked at a trailhead. This proposed Trail-Park system is intended to pay for maintenance of trailheads and is separate from the free wilderness permit described earlier.

FINDING THE TRAILHEAD

Here you will find detailed driving directions to the trailhead from the nearest large town with basic tourist services. This is normally the same town mentioned under "General location." For one-way hikes requiring a car shuttle, both trailheads are described.

KEY POINTS

This section is a brief mileage log of the hike, emphasizing trail junctions and other important landmarks.

THE HIKE

This section describes the trail or cross-country route itself, together with points of interest, natural and human history, geology, and other information of interest.

The Hikes

MOUNT JEFFERSON

OVERVIEW

This section covers the Mount Jefferson Wilderness and adjacent areas, including the Bull of the Woods Wilderness and the Olallie Lake Scenic Area. For many years, the Mount Jefferson region was one of the most unknown and inaccessible areas in Oregon. Early maps showed the mountain but little else. Even today, roads do not approach Mount Jefferson itself. The area was first protected as a National Forest Primitive Area in 1930. It became part of the National Wilderness Preservation System when Congress passed the Wilderness Act in 1964. The wilderness and surrounding areas encompass a wild variety of terrain, deep glacial canyons, whitewater gorges, magnificent old-growth forest, glacial lakes, alpine meadows, and towering peaks.

1 PANSY LAKE

General description:	A short day hike in the Bull of the Woods Wilderness through old-growth Douglas-fir forest to a lake set in a deep glacial basin.
Location:	About 58 miles north of Detroit.
Maps:	Bull of the Woods USGS; Mount Hood National Forest.
Difficulty:	Easy.
Length:	2.2 miles round-trip.
Elevation:	3,520 to 4,000 feet.
Best season:	Summer and fall.
Permit:	Permit required for day and overnight hikes; self issue at trailhead.
For more information:	Estacada–Clackamas Ranger District, Mount Hood National Forest.

Key points:

0.0   Trailhead.
0.8   Dickey Lake Trail junction; go right.
1.0   Pansy Lake junction; go right again.
1.1   Pansy Lake.

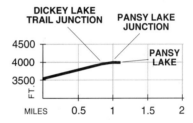

Finding the trailhead: From Detroit, drive northeast on Forest Road 46 about 41 miles, then turn left (south) on Forest Road 63, which is paved. Continue about 5 miles, then turn right (west) on maintained, gravel Forest Road 6340. Drive 8 miles, then turn right (southwest) on Forest Road 6341, which is paved. Continue 3.6 miles to the marked trailhead.

The hike: The Pansy Lake Trail plunges right into old-growth Douglas-fir forest; a welcome relief from the miles of clearcut timber along the access road. A gradual climb through cathedral-like forest leads to a trail junction. Stay right (south) on the marked trail to Pansy Lake. A short distance later, turn right again and walk a few dozen yards to the shore of Pansy Lake. The lake is small and shallow, but the setting is impressive. Pansy Lake basin is a nearly perfect semicircle of steep bluffs and cliffs with a classic glacial cirque. Looking at the flourishing forest, it's hard to imagine a huge mass of ice filling the cirque and grinding away at the mountainsides. Look closely on the return hike, however, and you may see how the valley below the lake has the characteristic U-shape of a glacial canyon.

Both side trails encountered on the hike to Pansy Lake can be combined with parts of the Bull of the Woods Trail (Hike 2) to form a loop hike. With a car shuttle, one could start at the Bull of the Woods Trail and make this a one-way hike to the Pansy Lake trailhead.

Pansy Lake.

PANSY LAKE
BULL OF THE WOODS

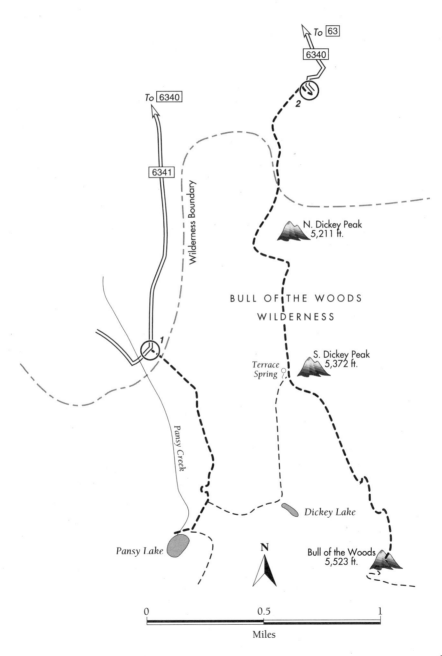

To 63

6340

2

To 6340

6341

Wilderness Boundary

N. Dickey Peak
5,211 ft.

BULL OF THE WOODS

WILDERNESS

1

S. Dickey Peak
5,372 ft.

Terrace
Spring

Pansy Creek

Dickey Lake

Pansy Lake

N

Bull of the Woods
5,523 ft.

| 0 | 0.5 | 1 |

Miles

2 BULL OF THE WOODS TRAIL

General description: A day hike to the second highest point in the Bull of the Woods Wilderness.

Location:	About 57 miles north of Detroit.
Maps:	Bull of the Woods USGS; Mount Hood National Forest.
Difficulty:	Moderate.
Length:	5.4 miles round-trip.
Elevation:	4,640 to 5,523 feet.
Best season:	Summer and fall.
Permit:	Permit required for day and overnight hikes; self issue at trailhead.
For more information:	Estacada–Clackamas Ranger District, Mount Hood National Forest.

See Map on Page 27

Key points:

0.0 Trailhead.
1.4 Terrace Spring.
1.6 Junction with Forest Trail 549; continue straight ahead.
2.7 Bull of the Woods summit.

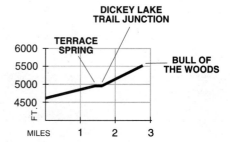

Finding the trailhead: From Detroit, drive northeast on paved Forest Road 46 about 41 miles, then turn left (south) on Forest Road 63, which is also paved. Continue about 5 miles, then turn right (west) on maintained, gravel Forest Road 6340. Continue 9.7 miles to the marked trailhead.

The hike: The Bull of the Woods Trail starts by climbing gently around a hillside through a clearcut, but within about 0.5 mile it enters undisturbed fir forest and passes the self-issue permit bulletin board. In another 0.4 mile it starts to contour along the steep west slope of North Dickey Peak. After passing through a saddle, it continues along the steep west side of South Dickey Peak. A sign marks Terrace Spring. Here and there, a few small talus slopes allow views to the west. A sign marks the junction with Trail 549 to Pansy Lake; stay left on Trail 550. (On the Bull of the Woods USGS map this junction is incorrectly located in the saddle south of South Dickey Peak.) Soon the trail regains the ridgetop and starts to climb. There are several points where rock outcrops allow good views to the east and north. A switchback leads to the pyramidal summit.

A fire lookout, more or less intact but no longer in use, stands on its short tower on the summit. The view is open in all directions, from the graceful

A succcession of wilderness ridges from Bull of the Woods.

summit of Mount Hood to the north to Mount Jefferson to the southeast and the Three Sisters to the south. Closer at hand lie the rugged, rocky ridges of the Bull of the Woods Wilderness.

3   OLALLIE BUTTE

General description:	A day hike in the Olallie Lake Scenic Area to a high summit overlooking much of the northern Oregon Cascades.
Location:	About 32 miles northeast of Detroit.
Maps:	Olallie Butte USGS; Mount Hood National Forest.
Difficulty:	Difficult.
Length:	6.4 miles round-trip.
Elevation:	4,640 to 7,215 feet.
Best season:	Summer and fall.
Permit:	Voluntary registration at trailhead.
For more information:	Estacada–Clackamas Ranger District, Mount Hood National Forest.

See Map on Page 34

Key points:
0.0   Trailhead.
0.2   Cross the Pacific Crest National Scenic Trail at right angles.
3.2   Summit of Olallie Butte.

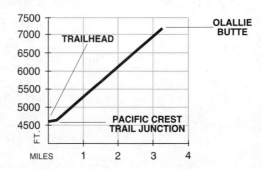

Finding the trailhead: From Detroit, drive about 22 miles northeast on paved Forest Road 46, then turn right (east) on to Forest Road 4690 at the sign for Olallie Lake. Continue 6 miles on this narrow, paved road, then turn right (south) onto gravel Forest Road 4220, also marked for Olallie Lake. Continue 2 miles to the point where two high-voltage transmission lines cross the road. Park under the second (south) set of wires in a pullout on the right. Cross the road; the unmarked trail starts on the south side of the powerline road.

The hike: The trail parallels the powerline for a short distance until it crosses the Pacific Crest National Scenic Trail (PCST). This junction is unmarked, but the PCST is marked both ways with small markers on the trees. Continue straight ahead (east). The trail wanders southeast, away from the powerline, up through the lodgepole pine forest, and ascends in broad switchbacks. There are occasional views to the northeast. About halfway to the summit, the forest becomes dominated by mountain hemlock and has a more open quality. Higher still, whitebark pine and subalpine fir start to appear. The trail crosses an open talus slope, and the trees hug the ground in the characteristic timberline appearance. A few short switchbacks lead to the broad summit area; turn left and walk to the top. The remains of a fire lookout are on the actual summit. The view is tremendous: Mount Hood to the north, the Cascade foothills to the west, Mount Jefferson, the Three Sisters, and Broken Top to the south, and to the east, the deserts of eastern Oregon. It's worth walking around the summit plateau to take in all these views.

It seems that every hill and peak in Oregon once had a fire lookout! In the early days of the Forest Service there were hundreds of fire lookouts in Oregon. They were needed to provide fire protection to the vast, remote country, which had very few roads. The lookout observer usually also functioned as a smokechaser; after reporting a smoke to the ranger station via telephone, the lookout would go to the fire on foot or by horse. Today, lookouts still provide vital early warning of fires. However, because of the vast increase in the number of roads, availability of aircraft for fire reconnaissance and attack, and mobility of fire crews, lookouts are used only for fire detection. Though fewer lookouts are needed, the key sites that remain are staffed by full-time personnel during the fire season.

Mount Hood from Olallie Butte.

4   FISH LAKE

General description:	A day hike to twoscenic lakes in the Olallie Lake Scenic Area.
Location:	About 34 miles northeast of Detroit.
Maps:	Olallie Butte USGS; Mount Hood National Forest.
Difficulty:	Moderate.
Length:	2.8 miles round-trip.
Elevation:	4,880 to 4,250.
Best season:	Summer and fall.
Permit:	Voluntary registration at trailhead.
For more information:	Estacada–Clackamas Ranger District, Mount Hood National Forest.

Key points:
0.0   Trailhead.
0.6   Red Lake Trail junction; stay right.
0.8   Fish Lake overlook.
1.3   Fish Lake.

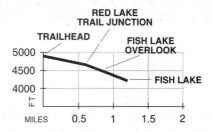

Finding the trailhead: From Detroit, drive about 22 miles northeast on paved Forest Road 46, then turn right (east) onto Forest Road 4690 at the sign for Olallie Lake. Continue 6 miles on this narrow, paved road, then turn right (south) onto gravel Forest Road 4220, also marked for Olallie Lake. After 5.6 miles, turn right into Lower Lake Campground. The marked trailhead is at the end of the small campground.

The hike: The trail climbs gently for a few yards then descends steadily to Lower Lake. It skirts this excellent little lake on the northeast side, then crosses the outlet stream to meet the Red Lake Trail. Stay right (northwest) on the Fish Lake Trail, which descends gently 0.2 mile to a scenic overlook. Fish Lake is in the foreground, and the headwaters of the Clackamas River spread out beyond. The only discordant note is the powerline, which marks the northern boundary of the Olallie Lake Scenic Area just north of Fish Lake. This viewpoint makes a good turnaround for families with children or those desiring an easy hike. If you decide to continue, follow the trail left and down several switchbacks to the south shore of Fish Lake. The trail skirts the west shore to reach the outlet and the end of the hike.

Forest reflections, Fish Lake.

OLALLIE BUTTE • FISH LAKE
DARK LAKE • PARK RIDGE

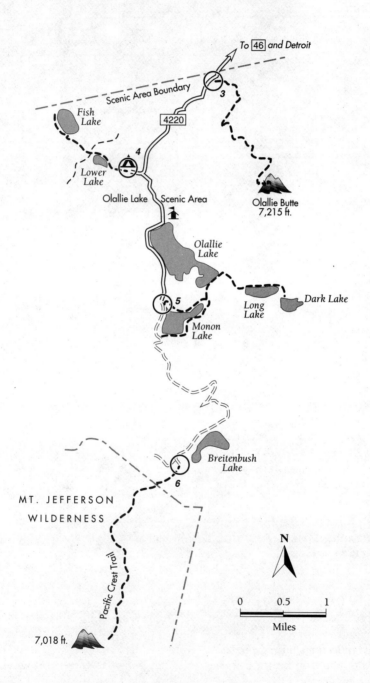

To 46 and Detroit

Scenic Area Boundary

Fish Lake

4220

3

4

Lower Lake

Olallie Lake   Scenic Area

Olallie Butte
7,215 ft.

Olallie Lake

5

Monon Lake

Long Lake

Dark Lake

Breitenbush Lake

6

MT. JEFFERSON
WILDERNESS

Pacific Crest Trail

N

0   0.5   1
Miles

7,018 ft.

5 DARK LAKE

General description:	A day hike in the Olallie Lake Scenic Area, featuring four alpine lakes.
Location:	About 36 miles northeast of Detroit.
Maps:	Olallie Butte USGS; Mount Hood National Forest.
Difficulty:	Moderate.
Length:	5.6-mile loop with a cherrystem (an out and back section).
Elevation:	4,960 to 4,700 feet.
Best season:	Summer and fall.
Permit:	None.
For more information:	Estacada–Clackamas Ranger District, Mount Hood National Forest.

Key points:
- 0.0 North Monon Lake trailhead.
- 0.3 South Monon Lake trailhead.
- 1.6 Olallie Lake junction; turn right.
- 1.8 Olallie Lake Trail; turn right again.
- 2.1 Long Lake Trail; go right.
- 2.5 Long Lake.
- 3.1 Dark Lake.
- 4.1 Olallie Lake Trail on the return; turn left.
- 4.4 Monon Lake turnoff; go left.
- 4.6 Monon Lake Trail; turn right.
- 5.6 North Monon Lake trailhead.

Finding the trailhead: From Detroit, drive about 22 miles northeast on paved Forest Road 46, then turn right (east) onto Forest Road 4690 at the sign for Olallie Lake. Continue 6 miles on this narrow, paved road, then turn right (south) onto gravel Forest Road 4220. Continue past Olallie Lake. About 19.5 miles from FR 46, you'll pass the turnoff for Peninsula Campground. Go another 0.3 mile to the marked north trailhead for the Monon Lake Trail, on the left (east).

The hike: Start by following the road 0.3 mile south to the south Monon Lake trailhead, then follow the Monon Lake Trail as it skirts the south shore of the lake. Lodgepole pine and mountain hemlock form the pleasant forest. The lakeshore is easily accessible from the trail, and you'll see a charming little peninsula with nice views of Olallie Butte reflected in the lake. Sections of the trail are built up with planks laid on crosswise logs to avoid boggy sections. The lake narrows as the trail proceeds northeast, but then opens out again. At the northeast end of the lake, turn right (north) on the trail signed for Olallie Lake. (The Monon Lake Trail, left, continues around the lake and will be the return trail.) The trail passes several small lakes, then reaches the Olallie Lake Trail. Turn right (northeast) and follow the

Weathered log, Monon Lake Trail.

trail along the southeast end of Olallie Lake. When you reach an unmarked intersection, turn right (southeast) and hike away from Olallie Lake. The trail descends slightly to reach Long Lake, then skirts its northern shore. The craggy summit of Mount Jefferson is just visible above the treetops to the south. Cross the outlet, follow the trail as it climbs a bit, then descend steeply to another intersection. Turn right and walk a few yards to some large talus boulders that have spilled into Dark Lake.

After enjoying the view, retrace your steps to the Monon Lake Trail and turn right (west). It's a pleasant, scenic mile along the north and west shores back to the north trailhead.

6 PARK RIDGE

General description:	A day hike to a scenic ridge in the Mount Jefferson Wilderness.
Location:	About 40 miles northeast of Detroit.
Maps:	Olallie Butte, Mount Jefferson USGS; Mount Hood National Forest.
Difficulty:	Moderate.
Length:	6.4 miles round-trip.
Elevation:	5,700 to 6,900 feet.
Best season:	Summer and fall.
Permit:	Permit required for day and overnight hikes; self issue at trailhead.
For more information:	Estacada–Clackamas Ranger District, Mount Hood National Forest.

See Map on Page 34

Key points:

    0.0 Trailhead.
    1.3 Unnamed saddle.
    3.2 Park Ridge.

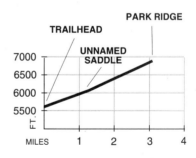

Finding the trailhead: From Detroit, drive about 22 miles northeast on paved Forest Road 46, then turn right (east) on to Forest Road 4690 at the sign for Olallie Lake. Continue 6 miles on this narrow, paved road, then turn right (south) onto gravel Forest Road 4220, also marked for Olallie Lake. About 19.5 miles from FR 46, you'll pass the turnoff for Peninsula Campground, and the road becomes rougher. With care, a passenger car can handle this section. In another 3.8 miles, you'll pass Breitenbush Lake Campground; turn left at the sign for the Pacific Crest National Scenic Trail parking.

Storm clouds surrounding Mount Jefferson.

The hike: Walk a few yards down the trail from the parking lot, then turn left (south) on the Pacific Crest National Scenic Trail. The trail wanders through alpine forest for a short distance, then starts to climb southwest through a delightful section of alpine meadows and parks. In fall, the meadows are a mix of colors as the ground-hugging plants turn yellow, orange, and red. Cross a footbridge and ignore an unmarked trail that branches right. The trail climbs through a saddle and turns more to the south. As the forest thins near timberline, a sweeping panorama of mountain terrain opens up. Working its way up though meadows and small stands of trees, the trail finally reaches a ridge crest at a small pond. It now follows the rocky crest toward a prominent high ridge ahead. The trail steepens somewhat to gain the top of the ridge and the end of the hike. (Of course, the Pacific Crest Trail continues, but this vantage point makes a great goal for our hike.) Jefferson Park lies in the foreground, a thousand feet below, and the imposing summit of Mount Jefferson forms the scenic backdrop. Much of the northern portion of the Mount Jefferson Wilderness is visible.

Mount Jefferson is a classic example of the fire and ice that has shaped the Cascade Mountains. The peak is a stratovolcano, built up from alternating layers of lava and ash. Lava flowed from vents during relatively quiet periods of volcanic eruption, forming a cone-shaped, gently sloping mountain. Other volcanic events were more violent, causing cinders and ash to be blown out of the vents. The eruption of Mount Saint Helens in 1980 followed this pattern. The initial explosive event scattered ash for thousands of square miles and was followed by fairly sedate lava flows.

While fire from the Earth's interior builds up the mountain, ice from the sky works to tear it down. There are five major glaciers on Mount Jefferson—rivers of ice that are present simply because more snow falls on the mountain than melts each year. As the layers of snow pile up, year after year, their weight compresses the lower layers into blue ice. The pull of gravity causes the ice to flow downhill like a river in slow motion. As it moves, the ice scours the bedrock and plucks away rocks that become imbedded in the ice. The glacier acts like a giant rasp, grinding away the rock and moving it downhill, leaving behind steep-sided, pyramidal peaks like Mount Jefferson.

The mountain was named for President Thomas Jefferson on March 30, 1806, by members of the Lewis and Clark expedition, who saw the peak from near the mouth of the Willamette River. Mount Jefferson, at 10,497 feet, is the second highest peak in Oregon and one of the most difficult to climb. The final summit pinnacle is the worst obstacle on the ascent. A party may have reached the actual summit as early as 1888.

7   FIRECAMP LAKES

General description:	A day hike in the Mount Jefferson Wilderness to the first of a series of alpine lakes.
Location:	About 18 miles northeast of Detroit.
Maps:	Breitenbush Hot Springs USGS; Mount Jefferson Wilderness Geo-Graphics; Willamette National Forest.
Difficulty:	Easy.
Length:	1.8 miles round-trip.
Elevation:	4,600 to 4,960 feet.
Best season:	Summer and fall.
Permit:	Permit required for day and overnight hikes; self issue at trailhead.
For more information:	Detroit Ranger District, Willamette National Forest.

Key points:

0.0   Trailhead.
0.9   Crown Lake.

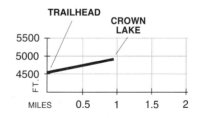

Finding the trailhead: From Detroit, drive northeast on paved Forest Road 46 about 11 miles, then turn right (east) on Forest Road 4685, which is gravel. Continue about 7 miles to the end of the road and the trailhead.

FIRECAMP LAKES • SOUTH BREITENBUSH GORGE
TRIANGULATION PEAK

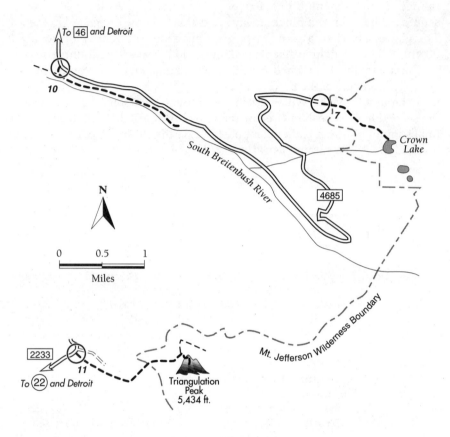

The hike: The Firecamp Lakes Trail starts in an old clearcut and follows an old logging track. Shortly, the trail enters undisturbed forest and the grade moderates. The trail reaches its high point about 0.5 mile from the start, then descends gradually to reach Crown Lake. The summit of Mount Jefferson looms over the treeline at the far side of the lake. Crown Lake is the first of three lakes that are collectively called the Firecamp Lakes. Most likely the name came from the use of the area as a base camp during an attack on a large forest fire.

Crown Lake.

8   BEAR POINT

General description:	A day hike to a peak in the Mount Jefferson Wilderness with views of Mount Jefferson and the Breitenbush River area.
Location:	About 15 miles east of Detroit.
Maps:	Mount Jefferson, Mount Bruno, Olallie Butte USGS; Mount Jefferson Wilderness Geo-Graphics; Willamette National Forest.
Difficulty:	Difficult.
Length:	6.6 miles round-trip.
Elevation:	3,180 to 6,043 feet.
Best season:	Summer and fall.
Permit:	Permit required for day and overnight hikes; self issue at trailhead.
For more information:	Detroit Ranger District, Willamette National Forest.

Key points:

0.0   Trailhead; start on the South Breitenbush Gorge Trail.

1.7   Turn left on the Bear Point Trail.

3.3   Summit of Bear Point.

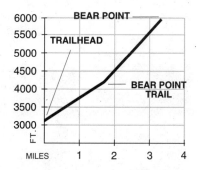

Finding the trailhead: From Detroit, drive east about 11 miles on paved Forest Road 46, then turn right (southeast) onto Forest Road 4685, which is gravel. Go 4 miles and park at the marked trailhead (it's where the road switches back to the left).

The hike: There are two trails at this trailhead; the South Breitenbush Trail is the one you want. If you're backpacking, pick up a copy of the wilderness regulations from the bulletin board at the trailhead. The first section of this hike is the same as the Jefferson Park hike (see Hike 9). After climbing steadily through the magnificent forest for nearly 2 miles, you'll reach the marked Bear Point Trail, shortly after the trail does a switchback to the left. Turn left

Mount Jefferson from Bear Point.

BEAR POINT • JEFFERSON PARK
WHITEWATER TRAIL

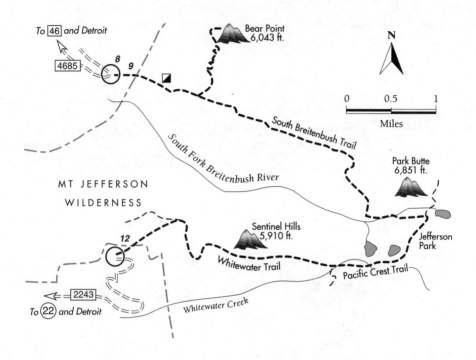

(north) and follow the Bear Point Trail through the fairly open forest.

At first the rate of climb is moderate, but the trail steepens as it reaches the open slopes. The small, patchy stands of trees were probably created by a large forest fire many years ago. As a result, the view is unusually good, with Mount Jefferson inevitably dominating the scene. More and more of the west half of the Mount Jefferson Wilderness becomes visible as you climb. Short switchbacks, and a lot of them, finally lead to the summit area. The last section of the trail swings around to the northwest side of the ridge before reaching the actual summit. The view is expansive in all directions, including the Olallie Lake Scenic Area to the northeast, and, of course, Mount Jefferson. Bear Point is higher than most of the ridges to the south, so many landmarks can be seen along the west side of the Wilderness.

9 JEFFERSON PARK

General description:	A day hike or overnight backpack to Jefferson Park in the Mount Jefferson Wilderness. Jefferson Park is a classic alpine meadow below the northwest slopes of Mount Jefferson. This hike provides excellent views of the glaciers on the mountain.
Location:	About 15 miles east of Detroit.
Maps:	Mount Bruno, Mount Jefferson USGS; Mount Jefferson Wilderness Geo-Graphics; Willamette National Forest.
Difficulty:	Difficult.
Length:	11.4 miles round-trip.
Elevation:	3,180 to 6,000 feet.
Best season:	Summer and fall.
Permit:	Permit required for day and overnight hikes; self issue at trailhead.
For more information:	Detroit Ranger District, Willamette National Forest.

Key points:
0.0   Trailhead; start on the South Breitenbush Gorge Trail.
1.7   Bear Point Trail junction; stay right.
5.7   Pacific Crest National Scenic Trail at Jefferson Park.

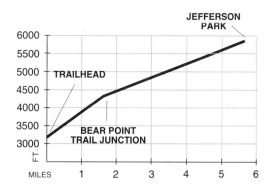

Finding the trailhead: From Detroit, drive east about 11 miles on paved Forest Road 46, then turn right (southeast) onto Forest Road 4685, which is gravel. Go 4 miles and park at the marked trailhead (it's where the road switches back to the left).

The hike: Jefferson Park, the destination of this hike, is very popular and heavily used. Camp in designated sites only. The area is closed to campfires; pick up a copy of the current wilderness regulations from the bulletin board at the trailhead.

The South Breitenbush Trail immediately attacks the nearly 3,000-foot climb to Jefferson Park, ascending steadily above the South Breitenbush

Mount Jefferson reflections, Jefferson Park.

River. It passes through a pleasant stand of Pacific silver fir for the first mile or so, crossing several small creeks. A ruined building stands right next to the trail, apparently a seeding shed used in reforestation efforts. The forest is thinner after this ruin, probably the result of a forest fire.

After the trail does a switchback to the left, you'll reach the marked Bear Point Trail junction. Stay right (east) here. Less than 1 mile beyond, the slope starts developing into a parklike bench, with many small, pleasant meadows. The views get steadily better as the trail continues its climb. As the trail passes several tiny ponds, its grade moderates. The highest point of the hike is reached as the trail swings across the head of a meadow at the upper end of the bench. It then starts descending along a somewhat more forested slope. Several switchbacks lead down a rocky section, then the trail crosses several pretty meadows. It turns south to skirt the south ridge of Park Butte, the 6,851-foot peak to the north, then turns east and enters Jefferson Park. Watch for several unofficial side trails in this area, which can confuse the route. The trail climbs gradually, and finally ends at a marked junction with the Pacific Crest National Scenic Trail.

It's certainly worth spending some time exploring Jefferson Park. The park is a classic subalpine meadow covering about 2 square miles. It lies near timberline, and the long, severe winters prevent the growth of thick forest. The trees tend to grow together in self-protective islands, favoring the higher ground in the hummocky terrain. Wildflowers prefer the lush, damp meadows. Numerous small lakes, a sure sign of glacial erosion, dot the park.

10 SOUTH BREITENBUSH GORGE

General description:	A day hike through magnificent old-growth Douglas-fir forest to a narrow river gorge.
Location:	About 12 miles northeast of Detroit.
Maps:	Breitenbush Hot Springs USGS; Mount Jefferson Wilderness Geo-Graphics; Willamette National Forest.
Difficulty:	Easy.
Length:	3.4 miles round-trip.
Elevation:	2,460 to 2,600 feet.
Best season:	Summer and fall.
Permit:	None.
For more information:	Detroit Ranger District, Willamette National Forest.

See Map on Page 40

Key points:
0.0   Trailhead.
1.7   South Breitenbush Gorge.

Bunchberry.

Finding the trailhead: From Detroit, drive northeast on paved Forest Road 46 about 11 miles, then turn right (east) on Forest Road 4685, which is gravel. Continue about 1 mile to the marked trailhead on the right side of the road. Parking is limited along the shoulder.

The hike: The South Breitenbush Gorge National Recreation Trail follows the South Fork Breitenbush River upstream through old-growth Douglas-fir forest. Several side trails lead down to the river, which is never more than a few dozen yards away. About 1 mile from the start, the trail passes through an extensive area of blowdown. Imagine trying to get through this section without a trail! In another 0.5 mile, a marked trail forks right and leads to South Breitenbush Gorge, our destination, in about 100 yards.

The gorge was probably carved at the end of the last glacial period, when warming temperatures melted the extensive ice cover in the high country and sent huge floods down the valleys.

11 TRIANGULATION PEAK

General description:	A day hike to a peak offering a view of most of the western Mount Jefferson Wilderness.
Location:	About 16 miles east of Detroit.
Maps:	Mount Bruno USGS; Mount Jefferson Wilderness Geo-Graphics; Willamette National Forest.
Difficulty:	Moderate.
Length:	5.2 miles round-trip.
Elevation:	4,750 to 5,434 feet.
Best season:	Summer and fall.
Permit:	Permit required for day and overnight hikes; self issue at trailhead.
For more information:	Detroit Ranger District, Willamette National Forest.

See Map on Page 40

Key points:
- 0.0 Trailhead.
- 1.9 Triangulation Trail, go right.
- 2.6 Triangulation Peak.

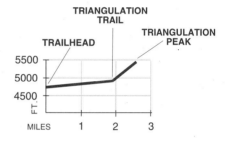

Finding the trailhead: From Detroit, drive about 6 miles south on Oregon Highway 22, then turn left (northeast) on Forest Road 2233. The road is paved for about 5 miles, then becomes gravel. Continue another 5 miles to the marked trailhead on the right, at the junction with Forest Road 635. Note that the trailhead is shown incorrectly on the Geo-Graphics and Forest Service maps. It is correct on the USGS map.

The hike: The trail follows the broad ridgecrest downhill to the southeast, then meets the edge of a clearcut. It follows an old logging road for about 100 feet then turns right and leaves the old road. After this, the trail stays in undisturbed forest and starts contouring around the steep north slopes of Triangulation Peak. About 1.5 miles from the trailhead, there is a good view of Spire Rock, a prominent rock tower on the north ridge of the peak. In another 0.4 mile, turn right on the marked Triangulation Trail. (The left fork continues to contour around the mountain.) Now the trail begins to climb steeply in a series of switchbacks, the first of which is right at the base of Spire Rock. It reaches the summit after about 0.6 mile.

The view of the western half of the Mount Jefferson Wilderness is excellent. Mount Jefferson itself is most impressive, sweeping up from the depths of Whitewater Creek to the glacier-carved summit. The view to the west is equally fine.

Mount Jefferson in late summer from Triangulation Peak.

General description: A day hike or overnight backpack in the Mount Jefferson Wilderness. The hike ends in Jefferson Park with close-up views of Mount Jefferson.

Location: About 18 miles east of Detroit.

Maps: Mount Jefferson USGS; Mount Jefferson Wilderness Geo-Graphics; Willamette National Forest.

Difficulty: Difficult.

Length: 11 miles round-trip.

Elevation: 4,100 to 5,900 feet.

Best season: Summer and fall.

See Map on Page 44

Permit: Permit required for day and overnight hikes; self issue at trailhead.

For more information: Detroit Ranger District, Willamette National Forest.

Key points:
- 0.0 Trailhead.
- 1.1 Junction with Triangulation Trail; stay right.
- 3.6 Go left on the Pacific Crest National Scenic Trail.
- 5.5 South Breitenbush Trail.

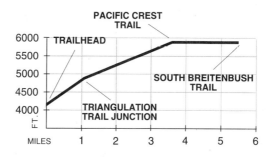

Finding the trailhead: From Detroit, drive southeast about 10 miles on Oregon Highway 22, then turn left (east) onto the marked, gravel Whitewater Road, Forest Road 2243. Continue 7.7 miles to the marked trailhead at the end of the road.

The hike: The Whitewater Trail climbs at a constant but moderate grade through Douglas-fir forest to the crest of the Sentinel Hills. About 1.1 miles from the start, it meets the signed Triangulation Trail in a saddle on the ridgecrest. Turn right (southeast) to remain on the Whitewater Trail as it continues to climb along the south slopes of the ridge. The grade eases as the trail swings around to the north slopes for a short distance. As it crosses a talus slope, there is a good view of the South Fork Breitenbush River valley. The trail passes through a saddle onto the steep south slopes and offers views

Hiking the Whitewater Trail.

of Whitewater and Russel Creek canyons and, shortly, of Mount Jefferson.

About 2.5 miles from the Triangulation Trail junction, the trail crosses Whitewater Creek on a footbridge then switches back up to meet the Pacific Crest National Scenic Trail (PCST). Turn left (northeast) at this marked junction. In about 0.8 mile, the trail reaches the south edge of Jefferson Park at the foot of the northwest slopes of Mount Jefferson. Turn left (north) on the PCST, which crosses the park from north to south. It's easy to find an excuse to linger and explore this beautiful area. Our hike ends at the junction with the South Breitenbush Trail, just before the PCST starts to climb out of the park to the north. With a car shuttle, you could combine this hike with the Jefferson Park hike, which follows the South Breitenbush Trail.

Jefferson Park is heavily used; be sure to pick up a copy of the current regulations at the trailhead bulletin board. The park is closed to campfires, and backpackers must camp at designated sites.

13 *MARION LAKE*

General description:	A day hike in the Mount Jefferson Wilderness with a loop along the shore of beautiful Marion Lake.
Location:	About 21 miles southeast of Detroit.
Maps:	Marion Forks, Marion Lake USGS; Mount Jefferson Wilderness Geo-Graphics; Willamette National Forest.
Difficulty:	Moderate.
Length:	4.6-mile loop.
Elevation:	3,350 to 4,150 feet.
Best season:	Summer and fall.
Permit:	Permit required for day and overnight hikes; self issue at trailhead.
For more information:	Detroit Ranger District, Willamette National Forest.

Key points:

0.0 Trailhead.
1.4 Lake Ann.
1.7 Turn right onto the Marion Outlet Trail.
2.1 Marion Lake; turn left.
2.7 Marion Lake Trail; go left.
2.9 End of loop at the Marion Outlet Trail; turn right.
4.6 Trailhead.

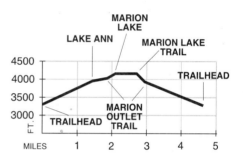

Finding the trailhead: From Detroit, drive about 15.6 miles southeast on Oregon Highway 22 to Marion Forks, then turn left (east) on the Marion Lake Road, Forest Road 2255. The road is paved for about 0.5 mile, then becomes gravel. Continue about 4.5 miles to the end of the road and the marked trailhead.

The hike: The Marion Lakes Trail climbs through a peaceful fir forest, working its way along the slope south of Moon Creek. It crosses the unmarked wilderness boundary after about 0.5 mile. About 1 mile from the trailhead, the trail climbs a steeper slope in a series of switchbacks, passing a couple of small springs. Soon the outlet stream of Lake Ann is audible from the right. The trail skirts Lake Ann on its west side, then reaches a marked trail junction. Turn right onto the Marion Outlet Trail.

Marion Creek, the outlet stream, is met at a bridged crossing at Marion Lake. Instead of crossing the bridge, turn left on the trail along the lakeshore. This trail rounds a point and turns northeast, affording views of the lake and the peak called Three Fingered Jack. At the northernmost point of Marion Lake, you'll meet the main Marion Lake Trail at an unmarked junction. Turn

MARION LAKE

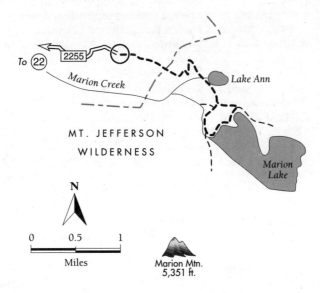

left (northwest) and follow this trail less than 0.5 mile to the junction with the Marion Outlet Trail. Turn right (north) to return to the trailhead via Lake Ann.

Marion Lake is popular, and signs of heavy use are evident along the lakeshore. Please respect the current wilderness regulations and stay out of areas that are closed for rehabilitation.

Marion Lake and Three Fingered Jack.

Coffin Mountain fire lookout.

14 COFFIN MOUNTAIN

General description:	A day hike to an occupied fire lookout, an alpine meadow, and views of both the Old Cascades and the High Cascades.
Location:	About 18 miles south of Detroit.
Maps:	Coffin Mountain USGS; Willamette National Forest.
Difficulty:	Moderate.
Length:	2.8 miles round-trip.
Elevation:	4,700 to 5,770 feet.
Best season:	Summer and fall.
Permit:	None.
For more information:	Detroit Ranger District, Willamette National Forest.

Key points:
0.0 Trailhead.
1.3 West Coffin Mountain trail junction.
1.4 Coffin Mountain.

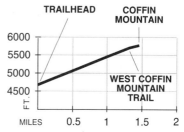

Finding the trailhead: From Detroit, drive east about 9.5 miles on Oregon Highway 22, then turn right (west) on paved Forest Road 11, the Straight Creek Road. Go 4.3 miles, then turn right onto Forest Road 1168, which is marked for Coffin Mountain Trail (ignore the first junction with FR 1168). Continue 3.9 miles, then park at the marked trailhead on the left (west).

The hike: Be sure to bring your own water for this hike; there is little shade on the hike. The lookout personnel cannot spare their water, which must be packed to the mountaintop. The trail starts out on a logging track, climbing steeply through an old clearcut. After a short distance it turns left and becomes a foot trail, working its way up the south ridge of the mountain. A few surviving trees shade this section of the trail, but soon it emerges into open meadow, the result of a forest fire.

At first it switches back along the south ridge, where the west-facing summit cliffs are visible above. Then it climbs across the meadow in several long switchbacks. As it regains the ridge, you'll catch a glimpse of the lookout building on the higher north summit. The trail enters a windswept alpine forest along the ridge and passes the junction with the "other" Coffin Mountain trail, which climbs up the west side. The lookout structure reappears, close at hand on its pedestal of imposing cliffs. Please respect the privacy of the lookout staff during the fire season when the lookout is in operation. The mountaintop is their home for the season. Unless they are busy, most lookouts welcome visitors. Ask permission before climbing the short flight of stairs to the catwalk.

COFFIN MOUNTAIN

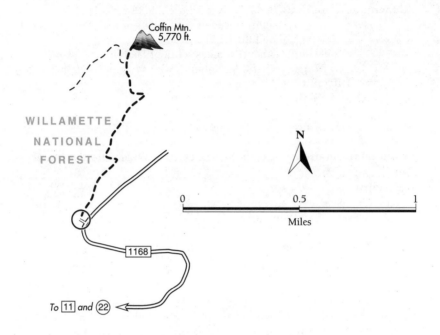

Coffin Mtn.
5,770 ft.

WILLAMETTE
NATIONAL
FOREST

N

0   0.5   1
Miles

1168

To 11 and 22

---

15   SANTIAM LAKE

General description:	A day hike or overnight backpack featuring two alpine lakes at the headwaters of the North Santiam River in the Mount Jefferson Wilderness.
Location:	About 30 miles southeast of Detroit.
Maps:	Santiam Junction USGS; Mount Jefferson Wilderness Geo-Graphics; Willamette National Forest.
Difficulty:	Moderate.
Length:	9.6 miles round-trip.
Elevation:	4,040 to 5,130 feet.
Best season:	Summer and fall.
Permit:	Permit required for day and overnight hikes; self issue at trailhead.
For more information:	Detroit Ranger District, Willamette National Forest.

Key points:

0.0   Trailhead.
0.2   Big Meadows Trail merges from left.
1.5   Porcupine Trail junction; stay right.
2.9   Lava Trail junction (to Twin Lakes); stay left to Duffy Lake.
3.2   Duffy Lake and first Santiam Pass turnoff; stay left.
3.5   Second Santiam Pass turnoff; turn right for Santiam Lake.
3.6   Third Santiam Pass turnoff; turn left.
4.0   Fourth Santiam Pass turnoff; turn right.
4.8   Santiam Lake.

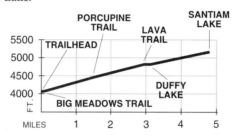

Finding the trailhead: From Detroit, drive about 26 miles east on Oregon Highway 22, then turn left (east) on Forest Road 2267, marked Big Meadows Road. Follow this narrow, paved road 2.6 miles, then turn left (east) onto a gravel road marked for Duffy Lake Trailhead. Go 0.4 mile and park at the trailhead.

Three Fingered Jack dominates Santiam Lake.

SANTIAM LAKE • MAXWELL BUTTE

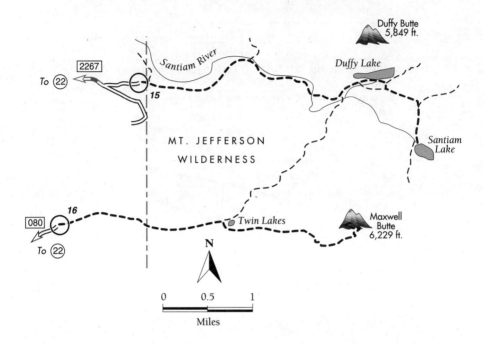

The hike: Starting behind the trailhead bulletin board, the Duffy Lake Trail contours to and passes through a low saddle. Here the horse trail from Big Meadows joins from the left (northwest). Now the trail starts to climb steadily, going east through a forest of large Douglas-fir and smaller Pacific silver fir, following the hillside south of the North Santiam River. As the trail climbs higher, more lodgepole pine are present on the drier slopes, and you'll also see mountain hemlock. Just past a talus slope on the right side of the trail, the Porcupine Trail branches left at a marked junction.

The Duffy Lake Trail climbs more gradually now and continues to follow the North Santiam River, dry in late season. Along this section of trail you'll start to see more subalpine fir, with its graceful, tapered, spirelike appearance. About 2.9 miles from the start of the hike, another trail branches right (southwest), this time marked for the Maxwell Trailhead. Remain on the Duffy Lake Trail and you'll reach the namesake lake in about 0.3 mile. This long, narrow lake is popular; camping is restricted to designated sites.

Near the southeast side of the lake, turn right at a trail junction marked for Santiam Pass. After just 0.1 mile, turn left at another junction marked for Santiam Pass. The trail climbs gradually for a while, then meets yet another trail junction for Santiam Pass. This time, turn right and continue about 0.8 mile to Santiam Lake, visible through the trees to the left of the trail. This fairly large lake forms an excellent backdrop for the craggy summit of Three Fingered Jack. For those who are backpacking, there are several good campsites north of the lake.

General description: A day hike or overnight backpack trip through beautiful alpine parks and meadows in the Mount Jefferson Wilderness. The summit of Maxwell Butte offers an expansive view of the southwest Mount Jefferson Wilderness.

Location: About 30 miles southeast of Detroit.

Maps: Santiam Junction USGS; Mount Jefferson Wilderness Geo-Graphics; Willamette National Forest.

Difficulty: Difficult.

Length: 8.4 miles round-trip.

Elevation: 3,760 to 6,229 feet.

Best season: Summer and fall.

Permit: Permit required for day and overnight hikes; self issue at trailhead.

For more information: Detroit Ranger District, Willamette National Forest.

Key points:

- 0.0 Trailhead.
- 1.9 Twin Lakes Trail junction; turn right.
- 4.2 Summit of Maxwell Butte.

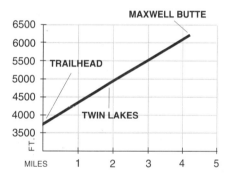

Finding the trailhead: From Detroit, drive about 29 miles east on Oregon Highway 22, then turn left (east) on Forest Road 080, the Maxwell Sno-Park road. Continue 0.5 mile past the snow parking area to the end of the road at a locked gate and the marked trailhead.

The hike: A short distance from the trailhead, the Maxwell Butte Trail starts to climb steadily eastward. It will continue at this same grade, with minor variations, to the base of Maxwell Butte. At first the forest is dominated by lodgepole pine, but soon Pacific silver fir becomes more common. Mountain hemlock makes an appearance about the time the marked wilderness boundary is crossed. After nearly 2 miles of hiking with no other landmarks, a marked trail forks to Eight Lakes Basin; turn right (southeast) to stay on the Maxwell Butte Trail.

The trail skirts Twin Lakes, a series of very shallow ponds that is the only permanent water on the hike, then resumes its steady climb. There are occasional glimpses of the butte itself. Less than a mile from Twin Lakes, the trail enters a series of alpine meadows on the west and south slopes of

Mount Jefferson Wilderness from the summit of Maxwell Butte.

Maxwell Butte. From here to the summit there is one great view after another. Subalpine fir form islands of forest in the parks. When the trail starts to switchback, it is a sign that the summit is near. A pile of rocks, melted glass, and some foundation piers are about all that's left of the old fire lookout, but the view is great without it. Mount Washington and North and Middle Sister dominate the view to the south, with Diamond Peak also visible. Mount Jefferson and Three Fingered Jack hog the views to the east and northeast. Closer at hand in the same direction lie three of the many lakes scattered through the west slope forest from east to north Santiam, Mowich, and Duffy lakes. To the west many of the summits of the old Cascades are visible, including the distinctive shape of Coffin Mountain.

17 CARL LAKE

General description:	A day hike or overnight backpack to a scenic mountain lake in the Mount Jefferson Wilderness.
Location:	About 25 miles northwest of Sisters.
Maps:	Marion Lake, Candle Creek USGS; Mount Jefferson Wilderness Geo-Graphics; Deschutes National Forest.
Difficulty:	Moderate.
Length:	8.2 miles round-trip.
Elevation:	4,540 to 5,500 feet.
Best season:	Summer and fall.
Permit:	Permit required for day and overnight hikes; self issue at trailhead.
For more information:	Sisters Ranger District, Deschutes National Forest.

See Map on Page 65

Key points:
  0.0   Trailhead.
  1.6   Cabot Lake; stay left
        on the main trail.
  4.1   Carl Lake.

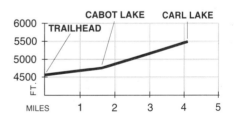

Finding the trailhead: From Sisters, drive northwest about 13 miles on U.S. Highway 20, then turn right (north) on Forest Road 12, marked "Mount Jefferson Wilderness Trailheads." Continue 4 miles on this paved road, then turn left (northwest) on Forest Road 1230, which is gravel. Go about 8 miles to the end of FR 1230 and the marked Cabot Lake trailhead. Follow the signs carefully at intersections; there are several sharp turns.

Rugged glacial terrain surrounds Carl Lake.

The hike: The Cabot Lake Trail starts out by contouring west along the south slope high above Cabot Creek, through a lodgepole pine forest with a few Douglas-fir. Watch for an impressively large Douglas-fir on the left not too far from the trailhead. The trail begins to climb gradually and offers occasional glimpses of the summit pyramid of Mount Jefferson. A short spur trail leads to Cabot Lake on the right, then the main trail starts to climb in several well-graded switchbacks. After only about 300 feet of elevation gain, the trail turns west again and climbs very gradually.

The forested basin features increasing amounts of Pacific silver fir and mountain hemlock, and becomes more open and parklike as the trail ascends. It passes several small, shallow lakes, then reaches the east shore of Carl Lake. After following the south shore to nearly the west end of the lake, the trail meets a junction with the trails to Junction Lake and to the Pacific Crest National Scenic Trail. This is the end of our hike, but it is worth exploring Carl Lake in detail. The south shore is easy walking and there is a gravel beach in late summer. The north shore is rockier and provides a rugged setting for this long, narrow lake.

CARL LAKE • ROCKPILE LAKE

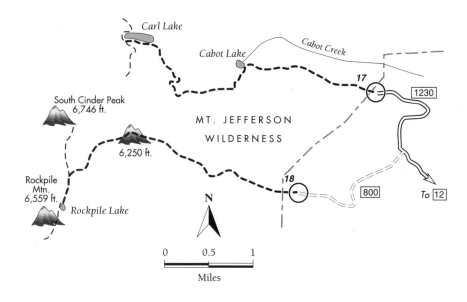

18 *ROCKPILE LAKE*

General description:	A day hike or overnight backpack trip to a high alpine lake on the crest of the Cascades in the Mount Jefferson Wilderness.
Location:	About 26 miles northwest of Sisters.
Maps:	Marion Lake, Candle Creek USGS; Mount Jefferson Wilderness Geo-Graphics; Deschutes National Forest.
Difficulty:	Moderate.
Length:	7.4 miles round-trip.
Elevation:	4,920 to 6,250 feet.
Best season:	Summer and fall.
Permit:	Permit required for day and overnight hikes; self issue at trailhead.
For more information:	Sisters Ranger District, Deschutes National Forest.

Key points:

0.0	Trailhead.
3.2	Pacific Crest National Scenic Trail; go left.
3.7	Rockpile Lake.

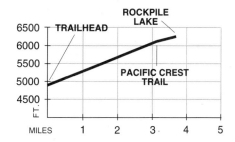

Finding the trailhead: From Sisters, drive northwest about 13 miles on U.S. Highway 20, then turn right (north) on Forest Road 12, marked "Mount Jefferson Wilderness Trailheads." Continue 4 miles on this paved road, then turn left (northwest) on Forest Road 1230, which is gravel. Go about 7 miles, then turn left (west) on Forest Road 900, which is marked "Brush Creek Trailhead." Continue about 2 miles to the trailhead at the end of the road.

The hike: This can be a hot, dry hike for the first 2 miles; there's no water along the trail until you reach Rockpile Lake. To start, follow the Brush Creek Trail as it starts to climb immediately. For the first 200 yards or so, a large clearcut borders the trail on the left. This unpleasant mess is soon left behind when the trail crosses the wilderness boundary. The trail climbs steadily and sometimes steeply, through a forest composed of mountain hemlock, lodgepole pine, Pacific silver fir, and subalpine fir. There are a few ponderosa pine at the trailhead. About a mile from the trailhead, the trail enters a recent burn. As the trail climbs higher, nearly all of the trees are dead from the fire. The views are great to the southeast and become even better when the trail reaches a narrower section of ridgecrest. Finally, the trail leaves the burn behind and traverses a beautiful area of alpine parks and open forest along the flat summit of the ridge. The ridge abruptly narrows, and there are dropoffs on both sides of this spectacular section. The trail goes through a notch and descends the south slope in several switchbacks. It then traverses the steep slope to the southwest. The forest here is typically alpine, containing mostly mountain

Rockpile Lake is perched on the Cascade crest.

hemlock and subalpine fir. The trail reaches an area of gentle slopes on the east side of the main crest and ends at the Pacific Crest National Scenic Trail. Turn left and walk about 0.5 mile to the north shore of Rockpile Lake. This small but deep lake is set in a superb location nearly on the main crest. There are just a few campsites near the lake; campfires are not allowed.

19 CANYON CREEK MEADOWS

General description:	A day hike to a series of alpine meadows in the Mount Jefferson Wilderness, with views of Three Fingered Jack.
Location:	About 25 miles northwest of Sisters.
Maps:	Three Fingered Jack, Marion Lake USGS; Mount Jefferson Wilderness Geo-Graphics; Deschutes National Forest.
Difficulty:	Moderate.
Length:	5.6 miles round-trip.
Elevation:	5,145 to 5,800 feet.
Best season:	Summer and fall.
Permit:	Permit required for day and overnight hikes; self issue at trailhead.
For more information:	Sisters Ranger District, Deschutes National Forest.

Storm clouds obscure the summit of Three Fingered Jack.

Key points:

  0.0   Trailhead.

  0.5   Go left on the Canyon Creek Meadows Trail.

  2.0   Canyon Creek Meadows; turn left.

  2.8   End of hike below Three Fingered Jack.

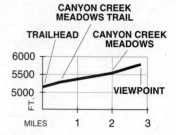

Finding the trailhead: From Sisters, drive northwest on U.S. Highway 20 about 13 miles, then turn right on paved Forest Road 12, marked "Mount Jefferson Wilderness Trailheads." Go north about 5 miles, then turn left on paved Forest Road 1230. The road crosses a bridge then becomes gravel. Continue about 1.5 miles on FR 1230, then turn left on Forest Road 1234, which is marked for Jack Lake. Drive to end of the road at Jack Lake Campground and trailhead.

The hike: Follow the Wasco Lake Trail as it skirts the east and north sides of Jack Lake. After passing the lake, turn left (southwest) on the marked Canyon Creek Meadows Trail. The trail climbs gradually through mountain hemlock and fir forest to reach Canyon Creek Meadow. Here a cutoff trail branches right; stay left and follow Canyon Creek uphill. Persevere up a last steep section and you will be rewarded when the trail reaches the broad, basin-like meadow below the spectacular northeast face of Three Fingered Jack. This alpine meadow is nearly flat and is fun to explore. The views of Three Fingered Jack are spectacular.

Three Fingered Jack is a stratovolcano, similar to its northern neighbor, Mount Jefferson, but more highly eroded. The glaciers that carved away most of the mountain are gone except for small perennial ice and snowfields, and the internal structure of the volcano is clearly visible. Alternating layers of volcanic rock are cut by dikes, the remains of conduits where molten rock once flowed on its way to the surface. Supposedly the mountain was named for a three-fingered trapper who worked the area. The difficult first ascent was made by six climbers from Bend in 1923.

CANYON CREEK MEADOWS
WASCO LAKE

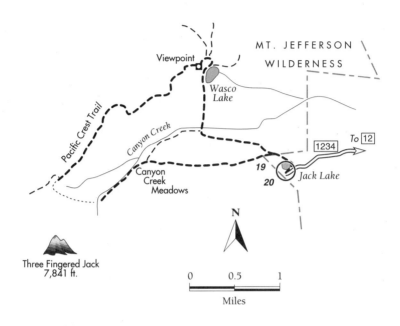

20 *WASCO LAKE*

General description:	A day hike, with an optional cross-country section, to a scenic viewpoint overlooking Wasco Lake in the Mount Jefferson Wilderness.
Location:	About 25 miles northwest of Sisters.
Maps:	Three Fingered Jack, Marion Lake USGS; Mount Jefferson Wilderness Geo-Graphics; Deschutes National Forest.
Difficulty:	Moderate (the optional loop is difficult).
Length:	7.6 miles round-trip (the optional loop is 10.3 miles).
Elevation:	5,145 to 5,400 feet (the optional loop reaches 6,360 feet).
Best season:	Summer and fall.
Permit:	Permit required for day and overnight hikes; self issue at trailhead.
For more information:	Sisters Ranger District, Deschutes National Forest.

Key points:

0.0	Trailhead.
0.5	Turn right on the Wasco Lake Trail.
1.6	Go straight ahead on the Wasco Lake Trail.
3.4	Go left on the trail to Minto Pass.
3.5	Turn left on the Pacific Crest National Scenic Trail.
3.8	Viewpoint and normal turnaround point.
6.6	Start of optional cross-country hike to Canyon Creek Meadows.
7.3	Canyon Creek Meadows Trail.
8.1	Go right, remaining on the Canyon Creek Meadows Trail.
9.8	Turn right on the Jack Lake Trail.
10.3	Trailhead.

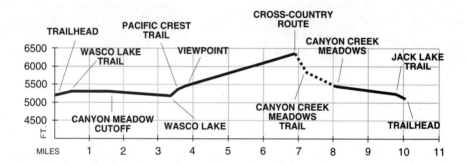

Finding the trailhead: From Sisters, drive northwest on U.S. Highway 20 about 13 miles, then turn right on paved Forest Road 12, marked "Mount Jefferson Wilderness Trailheads." Go north about 5 miles, then turn left (west) on paved Forest Road 1230. The road crosses a bridge then becomes gravel. Continue about 1.5 miles on FR 1230, then turn left (west) on Forest Road 1234, which is marked for Jack Lake. Drive to end of the road at Jack Lake Campground and trailhead.

The hike: Start on the Wasco Lake Trail, which goes north from the trailhead and skirts the east and north shores of Jack Lake. After passing the lake, turn right at the marked junction with the Canyon Creek Meadows Trail, remaining on the Wasco Lake Trail. The trail contours through mountain hemlock and fir forest, then crosses Canyon Creek at a nice little waterfall. It continues to Wasco Lake and skirts the lake on its west side. On the north side of the lake, turn left (west) on the marked trail, which connects to the Pacific Crest National Scenic Trail (PCST) at Minto Pass (the right fork goes to Minto Lake). A short, steep climb leads to the pass and a four-way trail junction. Turn left (south) on the PCST and go a short distance to an obvious rock rim with a great view of Wasco Lake and the Canyon Creek area.

Minto Pass is named after John Minto, who, in 1874, followed an old

Indian trail that led over the pass. The route became known as the Marion and Wasco Stock and Wagon Road. Although it was used for horse travel, a wagon roadbed was never constructed. Discovery of the lower Santiam Pass route to the south caused the abandonment of Minto Pass. Eventually, the Forest Service improved the Minto Trail.

There is an optional hike that makes a loop with the Canyon Creek Meadows hike. It involves a little over 0.5 mile of cross-country travel and will make the hike 9.3 miles. To do this loop, continue on the PCST as it climbs slowly up the broad, forested ridge to the south of the viewpoint. About 3 miles from Minto Pass, the trail crosses onto the east side of the ridge and soon breaks out of the trees for a great view of the north face of Three Fingered Jack.

To continue with the loop, first note the basinlike meadow below to the southeast. To join the Canyon Creek Meadow Trail, you will have to cross the meadow along its northern side and intersect the trail on the steep, forested hillside just beyond the meadow. Leave the PCST and follow the treeline downhill to the south. You will find some trail along here. When you cross the fork of Canyon Creek, turn more to the east and head down to the north edge of the meadow. At the east side of the meadow, climb a short distance up the steep slope to reach the Canyon Creek Meadows Trail. Turn left (north) to return to the trailhead at Jack Lake. See Hike 19 for details.

Wasco Lake from the Pacific Crest Trail.

General description:	A day hike or easy overnight backpack trip to a lake in the Mount Jefferson Wilderness, with a view of Three Fingered Jack.
Location:	About 12 miles northwest of Sisters.
Maps:	Three Fingered Jack USGS; Mount Jefferson Wilderness Geo-Graphics; Deschutes National Forest.
Difficulty:	Easy.
Length:	4 miles round-trip.
Elevation:	4,800 to 5,000 feet.
Best season:	Summer and fall.
Permit:	Permit required for day and overnight hikes; self issue at trailhead.
For more information:	Sisters Ranger District, Deschutes National Forest.

Key points:
0.0   Trailhead; go left on the Pacific Crest National Scenic Trail.
0.2   Turn right on the Square Lake Trail.
2.0   Square Lake.

Square Lake on a crisp autumn day.

SQUARE LAKE

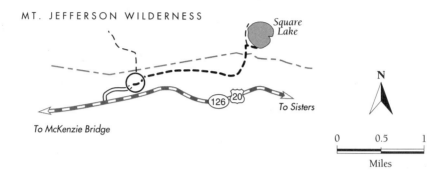

MT. JEFFERSON WILDERNESS

Square Lake

N

To Sisters

To McKenzie Bridge

0   0.5   1
Miles

Finding the trailhead: From Sisters, drive northwest about 12 miles on U.S. Highway 20 and turn right (north) into the marked Pacific Crest National Scenic Trail parking area. This trailhead turnoff is just beyond Santiam Pass.

The hike: Start out on the marked Pacific Crest National Scenic Trail (PCST). A few yards from the trailhead, you meet the actual Pacific Crest Trail at a marked junction. Turn left (north) and follow the PCST a short distance to a second junction. Turn right (east) onto Square Lake Trail. The trail climbs gradually along the south-facing slope through a forest of lodge-pole pine, mountain hemlock, and subalpine fir, which contains many dead and dying trees. Probably because the relatively open forest canopy lets in more light, the forest floor is more verdant than usual. After about 1.5 miles, the trail crosses a ridge and starts to descend, swinging more to the north as it does so. A sign marks the wilderness boundary, and shortly afterward the lake comes into view. At an unmarked junction, turn sharply right to reach Square Lake's south shore and a good view of Three Fingered Jack.

During the first section of the hike it's hard to ignore the sounds of the busy highway out of sight below, where traffic climbs the grade to Santiam Pass. The pass would be even busier if an early plan to build a railroad over the pass had been completed. The Corvallis Valley and Eastern Railroad built track from Newport (Yaquina Bay) to within 12 miles of Santiam Pass, and by 1887 parts of the line were in use. Construction was begun over Santiam Pass, but sparse settlement in central Oregon and the fact that two rival railroads had already reached Portland doomed the project to financial ruin. Parts of the old railroad grade can still be seen near the pass.

General description:	A day hike to the summit of a large cinder cone, featuring stunning views of the east side of the Cascades from Mount Jefferson to the Three Sisters.
Location:	About 17 miles northwest of Sisters.
Maps:	Black Butte USGS; Deschutes National Forest.
Difficulty:	Moderate.
Length:	4 miles round-trip.
Elevation:	4,880 to 6,436 feet.
Best season:	Summer and fall.
Permit:	None.
For more information:	Sisters Ranger District, Deschutes National Forest.

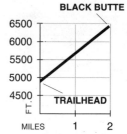

Key points:
0.0   Trailhead.
2.0   Summit of Black Butte.

Finding the trailhead: From Sisters, drive about 6 miles northwest on U.S. Highway 20, then turn right (north) on paved Forest Road 11. After 4.6 miles, turn left (west) on gravel Forest Road 1110, marked for the Black Butte Trail. Drive this road 5.4 miles to its end at the trailhead.

The hike: Black Butte is an immense cinder cone set well to the east of the main Cascade crest and rising 3,000 feet above its immediate base. The 6,430-foot summit has been used as a fire lookout since the early days of the Forest Service. It's still in use today, and hikers can view three generations of lookout structures. The hike is dry and can be warm; be sure to bring plenty of water. The popular trail starts climbing at a moderate rate and never relents until reaching the top. It first goes left, through an impressive stand of ponderosa pine. Note the large number of trees with parasitic mistletoe hanging from their branches.

As the trail swings around to the west side of the mountain, it suddenly enters a fir forest, dominated by grand fir. The trail switches back to the right and continues on this tack all the way to the summit. Watch for a few quaking aspen. There are also a few western white pine, many of which seem to be in bad shape. As the trail comes around to the southwest slopes again, the trees become much shorter, probably due to the harsh growing conditions here; hot and dry in summer and cold and wind-blasted in winter. Whitebark pines begin to appear in this area.

When the trail rounds the south side, you'll get a glimpse of the fire tower on the summit. The trail continues around to the east side before

New fire tower on Black Butte.

BLACK BUTTE

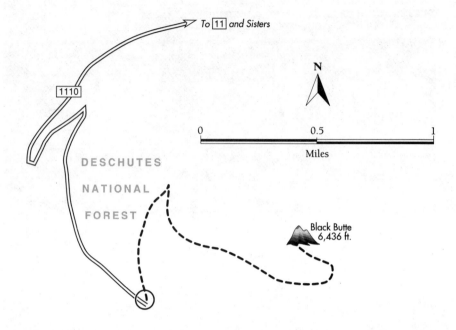

To 11 and Sisters

1110

DESCHUTES

NATIONAL

FOREST

N

0   0.5   1

Miles

Black Butte
6,436 ft.

reaching the top, which is dominated by subalpine fir. The first fire lookout you see is the current one, built in 1995. Continue along the trail to a second lookout tower, which has been closed for safety reasons. The trail meanders down to the oldest lookout building, a small square house with a cupola. Just beyond that structure is a newer log cabin, which is the lookout's residence. (Please respect the privacy of the lookout; the mountaintop is his or her home for the fire season.) The oldest fire lookout structure is long gone; it was a wooden platform attached to a couple of treetops. It would have been an interesting place in a thunderstorm!

The heavily eroded, jagged spires of Three Fingered Jack and Mount Washington stand in stark contrast to the nearly symmetric cone of Black Butte. At first glance it appears that Black Butte must be the younger mountain and therefore not yet eroded by glaciers. But geologists have determined that Three Fingered Jack and Mount Washington are younger than Black Crater. Why have glaciers not carved away at the slopes of Black Crater? The answer lies in the mountain's relative positions. Mount Washington and Three Fingered Jack are on the Cascade Crest and receive large amounts of snow. Black Crater, on the other hand, lies in the rain shadow, well to the east of the crest. Even during the ice ages, not enough snow built up on the mountain's slopes to form glaciers. A close look at Black Butte does show that its surface has been deeply eroded by rain runoff, which gives a clue to its true age.

23 *METOLIUS RIVER*

General description:	A day hike along the Metolius River.
Location:	About 20 miles northwest of Sisters.
Maps:	Candle Creek, Black Butte USGS; Mount Jefferson Wilderness Geo-Graphics; Deschutes National Forest.
Difficulty:	Easy.
Length:	4.1 miles round-trip.
Elevation:	2,760 to 2,840 feet.
Best season:	Year-round.
Permit:	None.
For more information:	Sisters Ranger District, Deschutes National Forest.

Key points:
- 0.0   Trailhead.
- 1.7   Spring on left bank.
- 2.0   Lower Canyon Creek trailhead.

Finding the trailhead: From Sisters, drive northwest on U.S. Highway 20 about 10 miles, then turn right (north) on Forest Road 14, marked for the Metolius River Recreation Area. Continue on this paved road about 10 miles, then turn left (west) at the Wizard Falls Fish Hatchery. Park on the left just before crossing the bridge over the river.

The hike: Much of the upper Metolius River is paralleled by hiking trails on both the east and west banks. This hike follows a segment of the West Metolius Trail. Cross the bridge, then turn left (south) on the marked trail. As you begin the forest is open ponderosa pine, but becomes shadier and dominated more by Douglas-fir as you continue upriver. The trail starts out on the pine bench above the river, but soon descends to the immediate river bank, where it remains. The beautiful, crystal-clear, rushing waters of the river, literally a step away, make this a special trail. About 1.7 miles from the fish hatchery, the river starts a sharp bend to the right. A major spring on the far bank gushes a massive amount of water into the river. In about 0.3 mile, your hike ends at the Lower Canyon Creek trailhead. Unless you've done a car shuttle, retrace your steps to the trailhead.

The Metolius River is only 35 miles long from the source to its confluence with the Deschutes River, yet it is one of the most interesting in the Cascades. Its historical course was abruptly interrupted near the headwaters by the eruption and growth of Black Butte. It appears that water that once flowed on the surface now percolates under the butte. The result is a dramatic and sudden birth of the river at Metolius Springs.

ADDITIONAL TRAILS

Opal Creek Trail starts from Forest Road 2209, west of the Bull of the Woods Wilderness, and goes up Opal Creek through old-growth forest.

METOLIUS RIVER

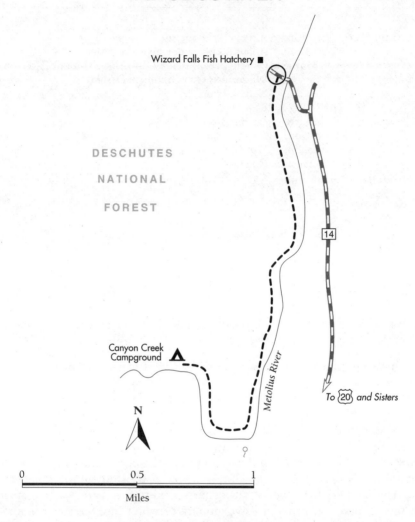

Wizard Falls Fish Hatchery ■

DESCHUTES

NATIONAL

FOREST

14

Canyon Creek
Campground

Metolius River

To (20) and Sisters

N

0   0.5   1

Miles

Phantom Bridge Trail starts from Forest Road 2207, north of Detroit, and runs generally west, ending at Forest Road 201.

Baggy Hot Springs Trail starts from Forest Road 4697 near Elk Lake, goes over the summit of Battle Ax, and north past Silver King Mountain to Baggy Hot Springs. A short trail returns to FR 4697 from Battle Ax, making a loop possible. Other side trails branch to Whetstone Mountain and Twin Lakes.

Elk Lake Creek Trail starts from FR 4697 at Elk Lake and runs down Elk Lake Creek to Forest Road 6300. Side trails go to Twin Lakes and Bull of the Woods.

Red Lake Trail starts at Olallie Lake in the Olallie Lake Scenic Area and goes to Red Lake; a side trail goes to Potato Butte.

Pacific Crest National Scenic Trail traverses the Olallie Lake Scenic Area from Olallie Lake to Breitenbush Lake.

Pyramid Butte Trail branches from the Pacific Crest National Scenic Trail south of the Breitenbush Lake trailhead and climbs to the summit of rocky Pyramid Butte.

Craig Trail starts from the same trailhead as the South Breitenbush Trail, crosses the South Breitenbush River at an unbridged crossing, and connects to the Triangulation Trail.

Devils Ridge Trail connects the end of Forest Road 670 to the Triangulation Trail.

Cheat Creek Trail starts from Forest Road 2243 and is an alternative route to the Triangulation Trail and the Whitewater Trail.

Pacific Crest National Scenic Trail runs the length of the Mount Jefferson Wilderness, from Jefferson Park to Santiam Pass.

Woodpecker Ridge Trail starts from Forest Road and joins the Pacific Crest National Scenic Trail west of Mount Jefferson.

Pamelia Lake Trail goes to Pamelia Lake, and spur trails go to the Pacific Crest National Scenic Trail and to the top of Grizzly Peak. Pamelia Lake is a limited entry area; permits must be picked up in advance of your hike at the Detroit Ranger Station.

Lake of the Woods Trail connects the Pacific Crest National Scenic Trail southwest of Pamelia Lake to Marion Lake.

Bingham Ridge Trail is a short spur trail off the Lake of the Woods Trail.

Swallow Pass Trail connects the southern section of the Lake of the Woods Trail to the Pacific Crest National Scenic Trail.

Blue Lake Trail connects Marion Lake to the Duffy Lake Trail.

Turpentine Trail parallels the Blue Lake Trail to the west, connecting the Pine Ridge Trailhead to the Duffy Lake Trail.

Pine Ridge Trail starts from the end of Forest Road 2261 and connects to the Blue Lake Trail near Marion Lake.

Minto Pass Trail connects Marion Lake to Minto Pass and the Pacific Crest National Scenic Trail.

Lava Trail connects Twin Lakes on the Maxwell Butte Trail to the Duffy Lake Trail.

Santiam Lake Trail continues south of Santiam Lake to join the Pacific Crest National Scenic Trail north of Santiam Pass.

Cabot Lake Trail continues beyond Carl Lake past Patsy Lake to Hole-in-the-Wall Park.

Jefferson Lake Trail starts from the end of Forest Road 1292 and connects to the Cabot Lake Trail at Patsy Lake.

Sugarpine Ridge Trail is an alternative to the Jefferson Lake Trail, starting near the same trailhead and ending at the Cabot Lake Trail north of Carl Lake.

Two Springs Trail starts from Forest Road 860 and connects to the Pacific Crest National Scenic Trail at Rockpile Lake.

Bear Valley Trail starts from Forest Road 1235 and also connects to the Pacific Crest National Scenic Trail at Rockpile Lake.

Two Springs Tie Trail connects the Two Springs and Bear Valley trails near their trailheads, making it possible to do a loop.

Minto Tie Trail connects the Bear Valley Trail to the Wasco Lake Trail near Wasco Lake.

Old Summit Trail starts at the Jack Lake trailhead and goes to Square Lake.

Round Lake Trail connects Round Lake to Square Lake.

Metolius River Trail runs the length of the Metolius River within the Deschutes National Forest, closely paralleled by Forest Road 14.

MENAGERIE WILDERNESS

OVERVIEW

The Menagerie Wilderness is named for the numerous small pinnacles scattered through the wilderness. Many of these rock formations are named for animals, and for that reason the area became known as the Menagerie. The rock towers were formed by differential erosion, when flowing water carried away the softer rock, leaving the harder rock standing. Because of these pinnacles, the area has been a popular rock climbing area for many years. Climbing here is challenging because climbers must often negotiate stretches of poor quality rock at the base of spires before reaching hard rock higher up. Unmaintained trails lead to most of the pinnacles.

24 TROUT CREEK TRAIL

General description:	A day hike to a scenic overlook in the Menagerie Wilderness.
Location:	About 67 miles northeast of Eugene.
Maps:	Upper Soda USGS; Menagerie Wilderness and Middle Santiam Wilderness USDAFS; Willamette National Forest.
Difficulty:	Moderate.
Length:	7 miles round-trip.
Elevation:	1,210 to 3,560 feet.
Best season:	Year-round.
Permit:	Permit required for day and overnight hikes; self issue at trailhead.
For more information:	Sweet Home Ranger District, Willamette National Forest.

Clearing storm from Rooster Rock.

TROUT CREEK TRAIL
ROOSTER ROCK TRAIL

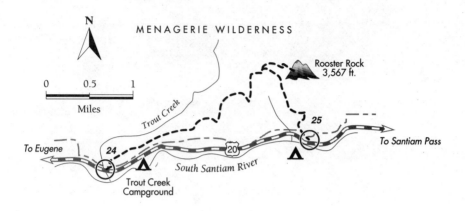

Key points:

   0.0   Trailhead.
   3.0   Rooster Rock Trail junction.
   3.5   Rooster Rock.

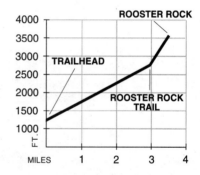

Finding the trailhead: From Eugene, drive about 23 miles north on Interstate 5, then go 19 miles east on Oregon Highway 228 to Sweet Home. Turn right (east) on U.S. Highway 20, then drive about 25 miles to Trout Creek Campground. The marked trailhead is on the left (north) just past the campground.

The hike: Due to the low elevation, this hike is open all year and is a good destination when the high Cascades are snowbound. The trail climbs gradually through the forest as it heads northeast. After about 1 mile it reaches the crest of the ridge above Trout Creek, then continues to skirt the southeast slopes of the ridge. The Douglas-fir forest is second growth; this area was devastated by a fire in 1870 and only a few old trees survived. After a couple of miles, the trail rounds a spur ridge and there are occasional views of Rooster Rock through the trees. After another 0.5 mile, the trail joins the Rooster Rock Trail; stay left and continue climbing as the trail steepens. The Rooster Rock Trail ends at a small rocky overlook, which is about level with the summit of Rooster Rock 100 yards to the south.

25 *ROOSTER ROCK TRAIL*

General description:	A day hike to a scenic overlook in the Menagerie Wilderness.
Location:	About 70 miles northeast of Eugene.
Maps:	Upper Soda USGS; Menagerie Wilderness and Middle Santiam Wilderness USDAFS; Willamette National Forest.
Difficulty:	Difficult.
Length:	4 miles round-trip.
Elevation:	1,320 to 3,560 feet.
Best season:	Year-round.
Permit:	Permit required for day and overnight hikes; self issue at trailhead.
For more information:	Sweet Home Ranger District, Willamette National Forest.

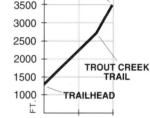

Key points:

0.0   Trailhead.
1.5   Trout Creek Trail.
2.0   Rooster Rock.

Finding the trailhead: From Eugene, drive about 23 miles north on Interstate 5, then go 19 miles east on Oregon Highway 228 to Sweet Home. Turn right (east) on U.S. Highway 20, then drive about 27 miles to Fernview Campground. The marked trailhead is on the left (north) about 0.1 mile past the campground. Park in the pullout next to the highway maintenance yard; parking is limited.

The hike: This trail is a shorter and steeper route to Rooster Rock. It starts climbing immediately, going north and northwest up a broad ridge. The forest is second-growth Douglas-fir. After about 1.5 miles, turn right (east) at the junction with the Trout Creek Trail. The trail climbs even more steeply for the last 0.5 mile. It ends at a rocky viewpoint overlooking Rooster Rock and the South Santiam Valley.

ADDITIONAL TRAILS

McQuade Creek Trail starts from Forest Road 1142 and climbs into the northwest portion of the Middle Santiam Wilderness, connecting to the Chimney Peak Trail.

Chimney Peak Trail starts from Forest Road 646 at the southeast corner of the Middle Santiam Wilderness and crosses to the northwest corner to end at Chimney Peak.

Knob Rock Trail starts from Forest Road 640 at the northeast edge of the Middle Santiam Wilderness and connects to the Chimney Peak Trail near its midpoint.

Middle Pyramid Trail starts from Forest Road 560, west of Oregon Highway 22, and climbs the middle summit of the Three Pyramids.

Crescent Mountain Trail starts from Forest Road 508, west of Santiam Junction, and climbs to the top of Crescent Mountain.

Browder Ridge Trail starts from Forest Road 1598, southwest of Santiam Junction, and traverses Browder Ridge to the west, ending at Forest Road 15.

Iron Mountain Trail starts from US 20 and climbs Iron Mountain. An alternate, the Cone Peak Trail, starts from US 20 farther to the east.

MOUNT WASHINGTON

OVERVIEW

The Mount Washington Wilderness is 52,516 acres and surrounds 7,794-foot Mount Washington, one of the most impressive peaks in the Oregon Cascades. More than 75 square miles of the Wilderness is covered by lava flows. Varied volcanic features make this one of the most interesting volcanic areas in the country. Numerous trails provide access to this stark and wild area, with the Pacific Crest National Scenic Trail being the most famous.

26 HACKLEMAN CREEK OLD-GROWTH TRAIL

General description:	A short, barrier-free day hike on an interpretive trail through old-growth forest.
Location:	About 28 miles north of McKenzie Bridge.
Maps:	Echo Mountain USGS; Willamette National Forest.
Difficulty:	Easy.
Length:	1-mile loop.
Elevation:	3,500 to 3,440 feet.
Best season:	Summer and fall.
Permit:	None.
For more information:	Sweet Home Ranger District, Willamette National Forest.

Key points:
- 0.0 Trailhead.
- 0.1 Start of loop.
- 0.5 Spur trail.
- 0.9 End of spur trail.
- 1.0 Trailhead.

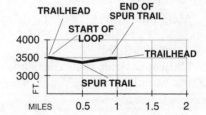

Old-growth Douglas-fir and seedlings on nurse log.

HACKLEMAN CREEK OLD-GROWTH TRAIL
ECHO BASIN TRAIL

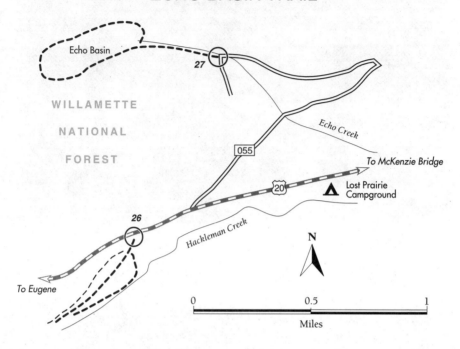

Finding the trailhead: From McKenzie Bridge, drive about 23 miles north on Oregon Highway 126, then go about 5 miles east on U.S. Highway 20. Just past Lost Prairie Campground, turn left at the marked trailhead.

The hike: This is an easy, well-built trail, worthwhile for a pleasant walk through old-growth forest. The trail is not shown on the topographic map, but an interpretive brochure is available at the register box. A short distance down the trail you'll come to a confusing junction; turn left, ignoring the old Santiam Wagon Road leading east, and turn back to the right. The trail leads through stately Douglas-fir and western hemlock, and numbered posts match the descriptions in the brochure. After about 0.5 mile, turn right at a T intersection and walk a few yards to an old road. This is what's left of the Santiam Wagon Road, a pioneer route opened in the late 1800s, connecting the Willamette Valley to central Oregon via Santiam Pass. For centuries, the pass was used by Native Americans to cross the Cascade Range. Trappers such as Peter Skene Ogden crossed the pass as early as 1825. Despite its low elevation, the steep approaches to the pass discouraged early wagon trail travellers who favored Willamette Pass during the 1850s. In 1859 Andrew Wiley and two companions worked out a route over the pass for wagons, and by 1866 the Santiam Wagon road was completed.

The barrier-free return to the trailhead is via the old road, but as an alternative, retrace your steps to the T intersection and continue straight. The trail makes a small loop at a point overlooking Hackleman Creek. From the east side of this loop, take a fainter trail that follows the creek downstream. This is the spur trail shown on the Forest Service brochure, which is not barrier-free. More numbered posts mark interesting areas. A main feature is the pocket of old-growth silver fir forest. The spur trail rejoins the main loop near the original confusing intersection. Turn right, then left, then right in the space of a few yards, then walk the short distance back to the trailhead.

27 ECHO BASIN TRAIL

General description:	A day hike to a mixed, old-growth forest.
Location:	About 30 miles north of McKenzie Bridge.
Maps:	Echo Mountain USGS; Willamette National Forest.
Difficulty:	Moderate.
Length:	1.9-mile loop.
Elevation:	4,160 to 4,800 feet.
Best season:	Summer and fall.
Permit:	None.
For more information:	Sweet Home Ranger District, Willamette National Forest.

Key points:
 0.0 Trailhead.
 0.4 Loop trail.
 1.5 End of loop.
 1.9 Trailhead.

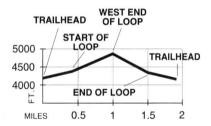

Finding the trailhead: From McKenzie Bridge, drive about 23 miles north on Oregon Highway 126, then go about 5 miles east on U.S. Highway 20. Just past Lost Prairie Campground, turn right on gravel Forest Road 055, which is marked for the Echo Mountain Trail. Drive 2 miles to the marked trailhead on the right (west) side of the road.

The hike: The trail climbs alongside Echo Creek through an old clearcut. Twenty-foot trees fill the old clearing now, and undergrowth crowds the trail. After about 0.3 mile, the trail enters the old-growth forest. At 0.4 mile, turn right (north) at an unmarked junction and cross the creek. Follow the trail carefully, since it is easy to lose where it crosses meadows. This glacial basin contains an interesting mix of noble fir, Alaska yellow-cedar, and Pacific silver fir. There are many young trees as well as old patriarchs, indicating that the basin was probably burned in a medium-intense fire that killed most but not all of the trees.

28 *PATJENS LAKES*

General description:	A day hike to scenic Patjens Lakes in the Mount Washington Wilderness.
Location:	About 20 miles northwest of Sisters.
Maps:	Santiam Junction, Clear Lake, Mount Washington USGS; Mount Washington Wilderness Geo-Graphics; Willamette National Forest.
Difficulty:	Moderate.
Length:	6.2-mile loop.
Elevation:	4,400 to 4,800 feet.
Best season:	Summer and fall.
Permit:	Permit required for day and overnight hikes; self issue at trailhead.
For more information:	McKenzie Ranger District, Willamette National Forest.

Key points:

0.0	Trailhead.
0.2	Go left on the Patjens Lake Trail.
1.5	Stay left at an unmarked junction.
1.9	Saddle.
3.5	Patjens Lakes.
4.8	Stay left at the cutoff trail to the Pacific Crest National Scenic Trail.
5.1	Go left along Big Lake.
5.4	Turn left, away from Big Lake.
6.0	Turn right.
6.2	Trailhead.

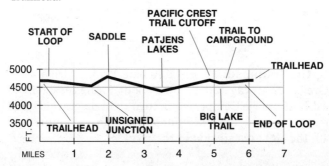

Finding the trailhead: From Sisters, drive northwest on U.S. Highway 20 about 13 miles, then turn right (south) on Forest Road 2690, marked for Hoodoo Ski Area and Big Lake. Stay on the main road about 3.2 miles to the marked trailhead on the right, just before entering Big Lake West Campground.

The hike: Shortly beyond the trailhead, the trail forks. Both forks are marked for Patjens Lakes; take the right fork. The other will be the return trail. The Patjens Lake Trail goes southwest down a gentle drainage through thick

PATJENS LAKE

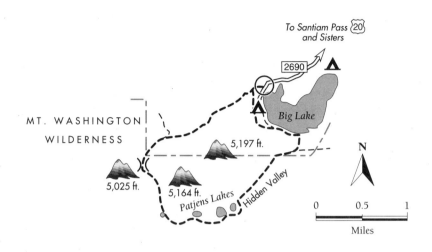

Cirrus clouds above the largest of the Patjens Lakes.

lodgepole-fir forest for about 1 mile, then starts to climb the slope on the left. An unnamed trail comes in from the right as our trail starts to climb. Be sure to stay left here. A short but fairly steep climb leads over a pass. The trail now turns southeast and descends into lower Hidden Valley, then wanders up the valley to the east to reach the first of the Patjens Lakes. The second and third lakes are a short distance farther.

Though shallow, the lakes are in a fine setting. A broad meadow surrounds both lakes and makes for pleasant walking. There are views of the unnamed ridge the trail just came over, as well as Mount Washington.

The main trail continues up Hidden Valley, climbing gradually, then comes to an unmarked trail junction. This trail forms a cutoff to the Pacific Crest National Scenic Trail. Stay left (north) and continue to the south shore of Big Lake, where the trail turns northwest along the lake. At the southwest corner of the lake, the trail forks again. The right fork leads to Big Lake West Campground; stay left on the Patjens Lake Trail. The trail climbs slightly, then descends to meet the outbound trail. Turn right to return to the trailhead.

29 CLEAR LAKE

General description:	A level day hike around a crystal alpine lake.
Location:	About 20 miles northeast of McKenzie Bridge.
Maps:	Echo Mountain, Santiam Junction, Clear Lake USGS; McKenzie River National Recreation Trail USDAFS; Willamette National Forest.
Difficulty:	Easy.
Length:	4.5-mile loop.
Elevation:	3,020 feet.
Best season:	Late spring through fall.
Permit:	None.
For more information:	McKenzie Ranger District, Willamette National Forest.

See Map on Page 95

Key points:

0.0	Trailhead at boat ramp.
1.6	McKenzie River Trail junction (north); go left.
2.7	Clear Lake Resort; stay near the lake shore.
3.9	McKenzie River Trail junction (south); turn left.
4.5	Trailhead.

Three Sisters from Clear Lake.

Finding the trailhead: From McKenzie Bridge, drive about 18.6 miles east on Oregon Highway 126, then turn right at the sign for Coldwater Cove Campground. Continue through the campground to the boat ramp, which is the trailhead.

The hike: Start at the marked McKenzie River/Clear Lake trail at the north side of the boat ramp. The trail leaves the forest after a few yards and crosses onto an open lava flow. (The trail is paved across the lava flow but is dirt elsewhere). The open terrain gives expansive views of the lake and a chance to look down into its remarkably clear water. The water is cold, only a few degrees above freezing, which keeps the lake low in nutrients and organisms. At the north end of the lava flow, the lake narrows and the trail enters old-growth Douglas-fir forest. Some of the firs are huge! Many of them bear fire scars, testimony to their ability to endure wildfire.

Shortly you'll arrive at a quiet pool, separated from the lake by a short channel. This is Great Spring, the source of Clear Lake and the McKenzie River. Watch the surface closely for roils caused by the volume of water welling upward. The trail continues around the pool and along the channel connecting it to the lake, where the motion of the water is more apparent. Where the trail returns to the lakeside, watch for ghostly trees and stumps underwater. These are the remnants of trees drowned when the lake was created about 3,000 years ago. This event occurred when lava from Sand Mountain flowed into the valley and dammed the McKenzie River. The cold water inhibits the growth of the organisms that normally would consume waterlogged wood.

Now, the trail leaves the lake to cross Fish Lake Creek on a footbridge. The creek is usually dry in late summer. Turn left (south) at the junction with the McKenzie River Trail, remaining on the Clear Lake Trail. The trail reaches the lake again at a viewpoint that looks down the narrows of the upper lake toward the glacier-clad peaks of the Three Sisters. Soon the trail leaves the lake to cross another drainage on a footbridge. Then it turns south along the west side of the lake and arrives at Clear Lake Resort. Follow the road closest to the lakeshore through the resort to a marked trailhead on its south side.

The old picnic shelter nearby was built by the Civilian Conservation Corps (CCC), a federal work corps active in the 1930s. Many campgrounds, picnic areas, and trails throughout the national forest system were built by the CCC. The quality and craftsmanship of their work is evident in the many trails and structures that still survive.

South of the resort, the trail follows the nearly straight western shore to the south end of the lake, where it crosses the outflow channel on another log footbridge. This is the start of the McKenzie River. On the far bank, turn left (north) at the junction with the McKenzie River Trail, which reaches the trailhead at the Coldwater Cove boat ramp in about 0.5 mile.

30 WATERFALLS TRAIL

General description:	A day hike along the McKenzie Wild and Scenic River, featuring two large waterfalls, numerous cascades, and magnificent old-growth forest.
Location:	About 19 miles east of McKenzie Bridge.
Maps:	Clear Lake USGS; McKenzie River National Recreation Trail USDAFS; Willamette National Forest.
Difficulty:	Easy.
Length:	3-mile loop.
Elevation:	2,610 to 2,940 feet.
Best season:	Spring through fall.
Permit:	None.
For more information:	McKenzie Ranger District, Willamette National Forest.

See Map on Page 95

Key points:

0.0 Trailhead at Sahalie Falls; go left, downstream.
0.4 Koosah Falls.
0.7 Trail to Carmen Reservoir; go right.
0.8 Carmen Reservoir; turn right, cross the road, then turn right again on the McKenzie River Trail.
2.3 Waterfalls Junction; turn right.
3.0 Trailhead at Sahalie Falls.

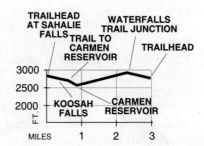

Sahalie Falls.

Finding the trailhead: From McKenzie Bridge, drive east on Oregon Highway 126 about 18.6 miles to the marked Sahalie Falls trailhead on the left (west). This turnoff is just past the Ice Cap Campground.

The hike: An easy trail with steps leads a few yards downhill to several fenced vantage points overlooking Sahalie Falls. The spectacular fall is about 100 feet high. Don't let the crowds of tourists put you off; you'll soon leave them behind. Turn left and follow the Waterfalls Trail downstream along the McKenzie River. Soon you'll come to a lower, broader fall; Koosah Falls. After about 1 mile, the trail forks. Take the right fork, which descends to Carmen Reservoir. The boisterous river becomes ominously quiet as it spills into the lake. The trail ends at a gravel road; turn right and cross the river on a bridge.

After about 100 yards, turn right on the marked McKenzie River Trail, which follows the west bank of the river upstream. You'll have views of numerous small cascades as well as Koosah and Sahalie falls from the opposite side. About 0.7 mile beyond Sahalie Falls, the trail crosses the river on a narrow footbridge made from a single large log. The McKenzie River Trail goes left at a T intersection; turn right (south) and follow the Waterfalls Trail downstream about 0.7 mile to the Sahalie Falls trailhead.

31 TAMOLITCH POOL

General description:	A day hike alongside the McKenzie River, leading to a beautiful pool where the river emerges from a lava flow.
Location:	About 13 miles east of McKenzie Bridge.
Maps:	Tamolitch Falls USGS; McKenzie River National Recreation Trail USDAFS; Willamette National Forest.
Difficulty:	Easy.
Length:	4 miles round-trip.
Elevation:	2,200 to 2,400 feet.
Best season:	Late spring through fall.
Permit:	None.
For more information:	McKenzie Ranger District, Willamette National Forest.

Key points:
   0.0   Trailhead.
   2.0   Tamolitch Pool.

Finding the trailhead: From McKenzie Bridge, drive east about 12.6 miles on Oregon Highway 22, then turn left at the sign for Trail Bridge Campground. Cross the river, then turn right on a paved road that leads past the power station

CLEAR LAKE • WATERFALLS TRAIL
TAMOLITCH POOL

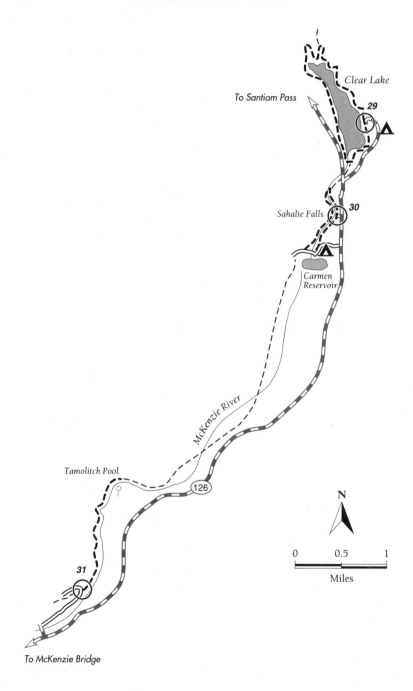

Clear Lake

To Santiam Pass

29

Sahalie Falls

30

Carmen
Reservoir

McKenzie River

Tamolitch Pool

126

N

0   0.5   1
Miles

31

To McKenzie Bridge

Fall foliage above Tamolitch Pool.

buildings. Continue about 0.25 mile to the point where the road switches back left; the marked McKenzie River Trail crosses the road here.

The hike: Turn right and follow the McKenzie River Trail north along the west side of the river. The pleasant, easy trail wanders through old-growth Douglas-fir and past western redcedar, distinctive because of its reddish, shredding bark and buttressed trunks. For the first mile or so, the trail stays close to the river, then crosses a side creek and climbs away from the bank. It works its way through hummocky lava, where the forest is less established and more open. Watch for several small, vertical lava tubes near the trail; one is about ten feet deep and two feet wide. These are tree molds, left when trees fell into the still-molten lava. Before the trunks burned completely, the lava hardened enough to retain their shapes.

The trail now follows the rim of a shallow gorge containing the river, which tumbles boisterously below. Suddenly you'll realize that the river is becoming quiet, a most un-McKenzie-like behavior. Shortly, you'll arrive at Tamolitch Pool. Meaning "bucket" or "tub" in Chinook, Tamolitch Pool is a beautiful cobalt blue. The entire flow of the McKenzie River surfaces in this pool, and the falls above are normally dry except during high flow levels.

About 1,600 years ago, lava flowed southwest from Belknap Crater (see Hike 34) and poured into the Tamolitch Valley. The lava is porous enough so that the McKenzie River is drained into the rock, and the bed is dry for about 2 miles, until the river re-emerges at Tamolitch Pool.

32   TENAS LAKES

General description:	A day hike or overnight backpack in the Mount Washington Wilderness, leading to several scenic lakes with glacial features.
Location:	About 21 miles east of McKenzie Bridge.
Maps:	Linton Lake USGS; Mount Washington Wilderness Geo-Graphics; Willamette National Forest.
Difficulty:	Moderate.
Length:	4.4 miles round-trip.
Elevation:	4,840 to 5,460 feet.
Best season:	Summer and fall.
Permit:	Permit required for day and overnight hikes; self issue at trailhead.
For more information:	McKenzie Ranger District, Willamette National Forest.

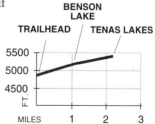

Key points:

0.0   Trailhead.
1.1   Benson Lake; go straight.
2.2   Tenas Lakes.

Finding the trailhead: From McKenzie Bridge, drive about 4 miles east on Oregon Highway 126, then turn right (east) on Oregon Highway 242. Continue 16.5 miles, then turn left (west) at the marked Scott Lake Campground turnoff. Go 0.9 mile on this potholed road to its end at the trailhead.

The hike: Before starting the main hike, it's worth checking out the views of the Three Sisters from the shores of Scott Lake. Back at the trailhead, follow the marked Benson Lake Trail as it meanders northwest through lodgepole pine forest. You'll also see subalpine fir, mountain hemlock, and grand fir in this alpine forest. None of the trees look very old, which is not surprising in this active volcanic area. After about 0.5 mile, the trail begins to climb, though never steeply. When it levels out again, watch for Benson Lake, visible through the trees to the left. The turnoff is unmarked. It's worth spending some time here, because the views change constantly from different points along the shore.

The main trail continues north, through forest now dominated by fir and mountain hemlock. Another, shorter climbs leads to the marked turnoff to Tenas Lake, on the left (west). It's just a couple of hundred yards to the largest of Tenas Lakes, which is a small but highly scenic rockbound lake. Some of the rocks bear obvious glacial signs in the form of striations. These long scratches indicate the direction of ice movement and are caused by rocks imbedded in the ice dragging over the bedrock. The scouring action of the glacier, acting as a giant rasp, digs out large depressions, which later become lakes, after the glacier has melted. The glacier also acts as fine sandpaper, sometimes leaving an almost mirror-like polish on the bedrock.

Tenas Lake.

TENAS LAKES
HAND LAKE

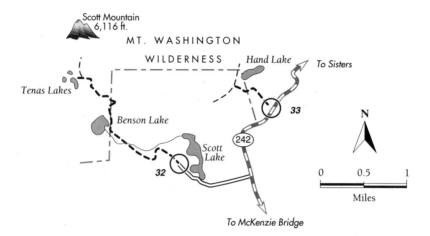

33 *HAND LAKE*

General description:	A day hike to an alpine meadow and a lava flow in the Mount Washington Wilderness.
Location:	About 21 miles west of Sisters.
Maps:	North Sister, Linton Lake USGS; Mount Washington Wilderness Geo-Graphics; Willamette National Forest.
Difficulty:	Easy.
Length:	2.2 miles round-trip.
Elevation:	4,740 to 4,800 feet.
Best season:	Summer and fall.
Permit:	Required for day and overnight hikes; self issue at trailhead.
For more information:	McKenzie Ranger District, Willamette National Forest.

Key points:
    0.0   Trailhead.
    0.6   Trail shelter.
    1.1   Hand Lake.

Finding the trailhead: From Sisters, drive west on Oregon Highway 242 about 21 miles and park at the trailhead on the south side of the road. The only sign visible from the highway is a small Forest Service hiker symbol.

Hand Lake meadow and Mount Washington.

The hike: The Hand Lake Trail starts from the north side of the highway, opposite the east end of the parking area and is marked. The trail descends slowly through a dense but pleasant stretch of forest. After about 0.5 mile it enters a large meadow. An Adirondack-style shelter is in a stand of trees on the right as you enter the meadow. The Hand Lake Trail crosses the meadow and climbs about 100 yards through the trees to fork both left and right. But the meadow is the interesting part of this hike. Its northern end is filled by a lava flow that looks as if it just stopped moving. It's worth walking around the small island of trees in the meadow just to have a closer look at the flow. Hand Lake itself is shallow and becomes much smaller in late summer.

34 LITTLE BELKNAP

General description:	A day hike across a moonlike lava flow on the Pacific Crest National Scenic Trail in the Mount Washington Wilderness.
Location:	About 17 miles west of Sisters.
Maps:	Mount Washington USGS; Mount Washington Wilderness Geo-Graphics; Willamette National Forest.
Difficulty:	Moderate.
Length:	4.4 miles round-trip.

Elevation:	5,200 to 6,305 feet.
Best season:	Summer and fall.
Permit:	Required for day and overnight hikes; self issue at trailhead.
For more information:	McKenzie Ranger District, Willamette National Forest.

Key points:

- 0.0 Trailhead.
- 0.7 Start of lava.
- 2.0 Go right at Little Belknap junction.
- 2.2 Little Belknap.

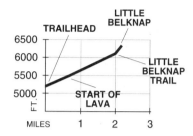

Finding the trailhead: From Sisters, drive west on Oregon Highway 242 about 17 miles, just past McKenzie Pass, and park at the Pacific Crest National Scenic Trail trailhead on the north side of the road.

The hike: There is no water on this hike, and no shade after the first 0.7 mile, so be sure you bring enough water. The trail starts out in a small island of cinders that supports a sparse forest of lodgepole pine and subalpine fir. After about a third of a mile, it crosses a few yards of lava flow to reach another, smaller island of trees. The trail takes advantage of the west and north sides of this island, but then strikes out across the bare lava.

Hiking the Pacific Crest Trail across the Belknap lava flow.

The trail climbs gradually, working its way around jagged heaps of gray brown rock. The going is surprisingly easy, considering the terrain. At first the lava flow seems entirely barren, punctuated only by scattered skeletons of dead trees. Soon, though, you start to notice life; lichen on the rocks, a clump of grass, a low alpine mat plant, and even a few white pine and subalpine fir seedlings. Though not enough to alter the moonscape feeling of the place, it's enough to hint at the tenaciousness of life. Given time, the plants will reduce the stark rocks to soil.

Ahead, you'll notice the bulk of Belknap Crater, and to its right a smaller knob with a reddish summit. The red knob is Little Belknap, our goal. As the Pacific Crest National Scenic Trail passes west of Little Belknap, watch for an unmarked junction. Turn right (east) and continue about 0.2 mile to the summit. The trail is good at first but becomes steep the last few yards. From the top, you're surrounded by a frozen sea of rock. The Three Sisters dominate the southern horizon, and to the north are the sharp summits of mounts Washington and Jefferson.

Mount Washington, the central landmark of the Mount Washington Wilderness, was first ascended by six climbers from Bend in 1923. Only 7,802 feet high, the peak is the exposed interior of an original volcano that was probably much higher. Glacial and water erosion have carved the present horn-shaped peak.

ADDITIONAL TRAILS

McKenzie River National Recreation Trail follows the course of the McKenzie River from its headwaters at Clear Lake to the town of McKenzie Bridge, closely paralleled by Oregon Highway 126.

Pacific Crest National Scenic Trail continues south from Santiam Pass, enters the Mount Washington Wilderness east of Big Lake, and passes Belknap Crater on its way to McKenzie Pass.

Pocket Way Trail starts from the old Santiam Wagon Road, Forest Road 3413, and connects to the Patjens Lakes Trail.

Trail 4050 starts from Forest Road 600 and wanders along the lower northeast slopes of Mount Washington, ending at Forest Road 690.

Hand Lake Trail continues from Hand Lake to the Robinson Lake Trailhead at Forest Road 2664 on the west side of the Mount Washington Wilderness. It also goes southwest to the Scott Lake trailhead.

Benson Lake Trail continues west beyond Tenas Lake to Forest Road 640.

Scott Mountain Trail leaves the Benson Lake Trail near Tenas Lake and climbs to the summit of Scott Mountain.

LITTLE BELKNAP
MATTHIEU LAKES

Belknap Crater
6,872 ft.

Little Belknap
6,305 ft.

Pacific Crest Trail

MT. WASHINGTON
WILDERNESS

To Sisters

34

36

McKenzie Pass

242

To McKenzie Bridge

THREE SISTERS
WILDERNESS

Pacific Crest Trail

N

N. Matthieu Lake

0   0.5   1

Miles

S. Matthieu Lake   Scott Pass

THREE SISTERS

OVERVIEW

The three prominent volcanoes that form the centerpiece of the central Oregon Cascades were shown on maps as early as 1859, but the origin of their names is unknown. At one time the three peaks were referred to as Faith, Hope, and Charity, but these names didn't stick. All three summits rise above 10,000 feet, and all are mantled with glaciers. South Sister is the highest at 10,358 feet. Depending on your vantage point, the summits stand out as clearly separate mountains or blend together to appear as only one or two peaks. Like many wilderness areas, the Three Sisters region was first protected as a National Forest Primitive Area. It became part of the National Wilderness Preservation System with the 1964 passage of the Wilderness

Act, and then was enlarged twice to its present size. It is the largest wilderness area in Oregon, at 283,402 acres. Many miles of trails and an excellent variety of landscapes make this one of the most popular hiking areas in Oregon.

35 BLACK CRATER

General description:	A day hike to Black Crater in the Three Sisters Wilderness. This summit offers a great view of the central Cascades.
Location:	About 12 miles west of Sisters.
Maps:	Mount Washington, Black Crater USGS; Mount Washington Wilderness Geo-Graphics; Deschutes National Forest.
Difficulty:	Difficult.
Length:	8 miles round-trip.
Elevation:	4,900 to 7,251 feet.
Best season:	Summer and fall.
Permit:	Required for day and overnight hikes; self issue at trailhead.
For more information:	Sisters Ranger District, Deschutes National Forest.

Key points:
0.0 Trailhead.
4.0 Summit of Black Crater.

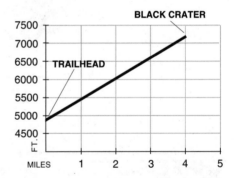

Finding the trailhead: From Sisters, drive west on Oregon Highway 242 about 12 miles to the Black Crater Trailhead, which is on the left just beyond Windy Point (the first lava viewpoint). Recently, a new trailhead has been constructed, greatly improving parking.

The hike: The summit of Black Crater probably is the best view of the Oregon Cascades reachable by trail. There is no water on this hike, so make certain you bring enough. The Black Crater Trail climbs very steeply right out of the trailhead, but soon starts switching back, which moderates the grade. The forest at this elevation is dominated by lodgepole pine and mountain hemlock, but as you continue to climb fir starts to take over. The forest also becomes much more open, which contributes to the uniqueness and high quality of this hike.

BLACK CRATER

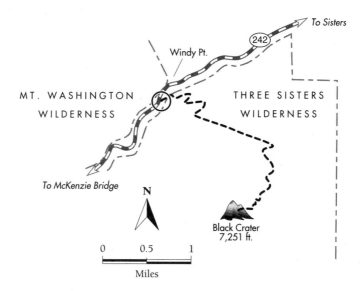

About 2.5 miles from the start, the grade lessens considerably as the trail crosses a broad terrace. You'll catch occasional views of the summit to the south. After this brief respite, the trail starts up the final summit cone (at about mile 3). It soon enters an area of open meadows and cinder slides with good views to the northeast. Steep switchbacks lead up through this area onto the summit ridge. The last 0.3 mile is a pleasant walk along the summit ridge to the peak.

Foundation bolts and other debris attest to the former presence of a Forest Service fire lookout. As with many others in Oregon, it has long since been removed. The views are truly stunning. To the northwest and north, the low cinder cones of Scott Mountain and Belknap Crater are visible, followed by the impressive spire of Mount Washington, and the snowy cones of mounts Jefferson and Hood. To the south, very close at hand, loom the Three Sisters and Broken Top. To the west, the flood of lava around the McKenzie Pass area attests to the violent volcanic history of the Cascades.

From this lofty vantage point, it seems incredible that anyone would attempt to build a road across the lava fields. Actually, the McKenzie Pass Road was the second wagon route built across this region of the high Cascades. (For details on the first, see Hike 36.) The approximate route of the present highway was discovered in 1866. By 1871, the road was operating as a toll road, at least after the deep snows of winter melted away. The wagon company won a valuable contract to carry the U.S. Mail. In an attempt to keep the mail moving during the winter, John Craig, one of the pioneers who worked

Mounts Jefferson and Hood from Black Crater.

on the early wagon road, attempted to ski across McKenzie Pass with a mail sack during the winter of 1877-78. He never made it. A monument along the highway west of the pass honors him.

As late as 1924, travel over the McKenzie Pass Highway was still difficult. Autos had to creep along at five miles per hour, and the lava rapidly wore out tires. Heavy snows still close the road in the winter. Some thought was given to keeping the highway open all year, but Santiam Pass proved to be a more practical route for an all-weather highway.

36 MATTHIEU LAKES

General description:	A day hike to a historic mountain pass in the Three Sisters Wilderness.
Location:	About 11 miles west of Sisters.
Maps:	North Sister USGS; Mount Washington Wilderness Geo-Graphics; Deschutes National Forest.
Difficulty:	Moderate.
Length:	5.2-mile loop.
Elevation:	5,320 to 6,040 feet.
Best season:	Summer and fall.
Permit:	Required for day and overnight hikes; self issue at trailhead.
For more information:	Sisters Ranger District, Deschutes National Forest.

See Map on Page 103

Key points:

0.0 Lava Camp trailhead.
0.2 Turn left on the Pacific Crest National Scenic Trail.
0.8 Matthieu Lake Trail; go right.
1.9 North Matthieu Lake.
2.5 Turn right on the Pacific Crest National Scenic Trail
2.6 South Matthieu Lake.

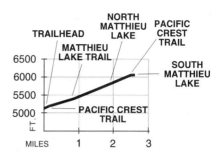

Finding the trailhead: From Sisters, drive west about 11 miles on Oregon Highway 242, then turn left (south) on the marked gravel road to Lava Camp Lake. After about 0.4 mile, turn right at the sign for the Pacific Crest National Scenic Trail.

The hike: There are two trails leaving this trailhead. Take the one on the right (west) that is marked "PCNST 1/2." At the junction with the Pacific Crest National Scenic Trail (PCST) turn left. The trail climbs slowly alongside the edge of a massive lava flow. After about 0.5 mile, turn right on the marked trail for North Matthieu Lake. The PCST goes left and is the return route.

The trail continues to follow the eastern edge of the lava flow for another 0.5 mile, then climbs more steeply, with a couple of switchbacks, to reach the bench that holds North Matthieu Lake. The lava flow makes a rugged backdrop for this small lake. Beyond, the trail gradually climbs the slope east of the lava flow to join the PCST, about 2 miles from the junction where we left it. Turn right and go a few yards to South Matthieu Lake, a small, potholelike lake right on the main Cascade Crest. Follow the trail around the east side of the lake to Scott Pass and the junction with the Scott Trail. This pass is our destination.

Scott Pass was named for Felix and Marion Scott, pioneers who, with 50 men, laid out a wagon road over this pass in 1862. From Scott Lake to the west, the route climbed the steep, jagged lava flows, turned north to reach the crest at South Matthieu Lake, then descended to Trout Creek on the east. Several wagon companies were formed to exploit the new route, but the discovery of the lower route now followed by the McKenzie Pass Highway put an end to interest in Scott Pass.

Retrace your steps to the Matthieu Lake Trail junction, then stay right to remain on the PCST. This trail stays high on the slopes for about 1 mile, with great views of the lava flow to the west. Notice also the interesting mix of trees on this dry, west-facing slope. There are lodgepole pine, mountain hemlock, subalpine fir, and ponderosa pine all growing together. After a while, the forest grows thicker, and the trail descends to meet the Matthieu Lakes Trail again. Go right to remain on the PCST and retrace your steps. In about 0.5 mile, turn right again at the trail junction marked "Lava Camp TH."

Lava flow and South Matthieu Lake.

37 THREE SISTERS

General description: A classic four-day or longer backpack around the Three Sisters peaks in the Three Sisters Wilderness. This alpine hike stays near timberline for most of the route.

Location: About 11 miles west of Sisters.

Maps: Mount Washington, North Sister, South Sister, Broken Top, Trout Creek Butte USGS; Three Sisters Wilderness Geo-Graphics; Willamette National Forest, Deschutes National Forest.

Difficulty: Difficult.

Length: 42.8-mile loop.

Elevation: 5,300 to 7,040 feet.

Best season: Summer and fall.

Permit: Required for day and overnight hikes; self issue at trailhead.

For more information: Sisters and Bend-Fort Rock ranger districts, Deschutes National Forest; McKenzie Ranger District, Willamette National Forest.

North Sister.

Key points:

- 0.0 Lava Camp trailhead.
- 0.2 Turn left on the PCST.
- 0.8 Go right on the Matthieu Lake Trail.
- 1.9 North Matthieu Lake.
- 2.5 PCST; turn right.
- 2.6 Scott Pass; stay right on the PCST.
- 4.8 Scott Trail (west); stay left on the PCST.
- 6.2 Opie Dilldock Pass.
- 8.5 Glacier Creek.
- 9.5 Sister Spring.
- 9.8 Obsidian Way Trail; stay left on the PCST.
- 11.6 Linton Meadow Trail (north); stay left on the PCST.
- 16.8 Linton Meadow Trail (south); stay left on the PCST.
- 17.1 Mesa Creek.
- 19.0 Go left on the cutoff trail to Moraine Lake Trail, leaving the PCST.
- 20.2 Moraine Lake Trail; turn left.
- 21.9 Moraine Lake.
- 22.9 Go left at Fall Creek.
- 24.9 Green Lakes; turn right then left to stay on Green Lakes Trail.
- 26.4 Pass.
- 28.6 Turn left on the Pole Creek Trail in Park Meadow.
- 31.0 South Fork Squaw Creek.
- 32.4 Chambers Lake Trail/Soap Creek; continue straight ahead.
- 33.0 Turn left, leaving the Pole Creek Trail.
- 36.7 Alder Creek.
- 38.7 Scott Trail; go left at this T intersection.
- 40.3 Scott Pass; turn right on the PCST.
- 40.4 Matthieu Lake Trail (south); stay right on the PCST.
- 42.0 Matthieu Lake Trail (north); stay right on the PCST.
- 42.6 Go right on the Lava Camp Trail, leaving the PCST.
- 42.8 Lava Camp trailhead.

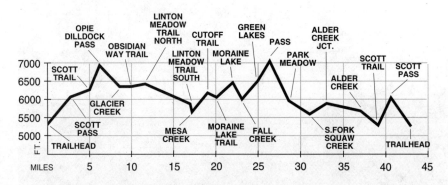

Finding the trailhead: From Sisters, drive west about 11 miles on Oregon Highway 242, then turn left (south) on the marked gravel road to Lava Camp Lake. After about 0.4 mile, turn right at the sign for the Pacific Crest National Scenic Trail (PCST).

THREE SISTERS

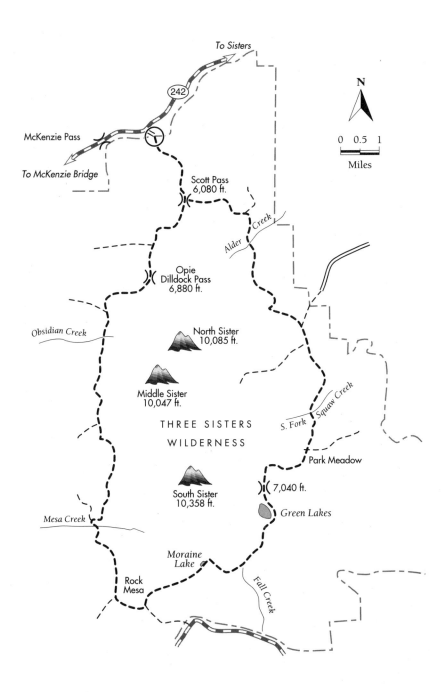

To Sisters

242

McKenzie Pass

To McKenzie Bridge

N

0   0.5   1
Miles

Scott Pass
6,080 ft.

Alder Creek

Opie
Dilldock Pass
6,880 ft.

Obsidian Creek

North Sister
10,085 ft.

Middle Sister
10,047 ft.

THREE SISTERS

WILDERNESS

S. Fork Squaw Creek

Park Meadow

South Sister
10,358 ft.

7,040 ft.

Green Lakes

Mesa Creek

Moraine
Lake

Rock
Mesa

Fall Creek

The hike: This hike starts and ends on the trails used by the Matthieu Lakes hike (see Hike 36). There are two trails leaving this trailhead. Take the one on the right (west), which is marked "PCNST 1/2." After about 0.2 mile, turn left (south) on the marked PCST. After about 0.6 mile, turn right (south) on the trail to South Matthieu Lake. After passing the lake, follow the trail as it climbs to meet the PCST near South Matthieu Lake. This small lake is located in Scott Pass. Camping within 250 feet of either lake is allowed in designated sites only, and campfires are not allowed.

Walk around the east side of South Matthieu Lake to the junction with the Scott Trail, which branches left. This will be your return trail. For now, stay with the PCST, which forks right (southwest). The well-constructed trail soon starts across a rugged lava flow, climbing gradually and working its way toward Yapoah Crater, a reddish cinder cone visible ahead. As the trail rounds the south slopes of the crater, the view opens up to the north, revealing the summits of Mount Washington, Three Finger Jack, Mount Jefferson, Mount Hood, and, barely, Mount Rainier. The trail skirts another tongue of lava, then drops slightly to enter a dry meadow. The Scott Trail branches left; go straight ahead (south) on the PCST. After climbing the slopes at the head of the valley, the trail reaches Minnie Scott Spring, a small but welcome source of water in this dry landscape after the snow melts. There is good camping on the flat ridge northwest of the spring.

Next the trail passes the northwest slopes of Collier Cone, a eroded cinder cone with several unmarked trails leading to the crest, and views of Collier Glacier on the northwest slopes of Middle Sister. Turning abruptly west, the PCST crosses onto another lava flow, reaching 6,880 feet at Opie Dilldock Pass. The pass is really just the high point in this section of trail. Now the trail descends a steep valley in the lava, switching back down several hundred feet until it finds a way around the cliff to the south. Once the trail reaches the forest, it parallels the lava flow for about 0.5 mile before turning south and contouring across the slope. At Glacier Creek, the PCST meets the Glacier Way Trail; continue south on the PCST.

As the trail climbs above the lush meadow, you'll start to notice glittering black obsidian—volcanic glass. This area contains an incredible amount of nearly pure obsidian. Soon the trail levels out and crosses a open, nearly level bench with several small ponds. Sister Spring marks the start of Obsidian Creek, which soon plunges over a waterfall next to the trail. The trail continues to descend below the falls and passes the junction with the Obsidian Way Trail.

The Obsidian area is a limited entry area. Hikers are required to have a limited entry permit if they plan to camp here. This permit must be obtained in advance at the McKenzie Ranger Station. If you're doing this hike as described, you don't need a permit as long as you don't camp within the Obsidian area.

For the next several miles, the PCST works its way south just at timberline. There are great views of all three Sisters as the trail contours through this beautiful landscape. In late season there are no water sources until reaching Separation Creek. The trail gradually descends, finally passing a small heart-shaped lake on its right before following Separation Creek for a short distance through a meadow. It crosses the head of Hinton Creek, then traverses the foot of a steep slope before making a descent to Mesa Creek. The meadow here has a number of good campsites along the south edge.

Re-entering the forest, the PCST is flat for a short distance. After it crosses another tributary of Mesa Creek it climbs several hundred feet in a large switchback, then enters a small alpine meadow. A more gentle section leads to a pass next to the imposing bulk of Rock Mesa, a large, glassy lava flow. The trail follows the edge of the lava southward across open Wickiup Plain; after about 0.5 mile, turn left (southeast) on a cutoff trail marked for Moraine Lake. This trail skirts the forested slopes of Le Conte Crater, then meets the Moraine Lake Trail at the southeast corner of Wickiup Plain. Turn left (northeast) and start climbing.

The trail levels out after about 250 feet of vertical and crosses onto another plain, skirting the forest north of Kaleetan Butte. Another forested climb of about 200 feet leads to views of Broken Top peak to the northeast. Cross the South Sister climber's trail and continue northeast as the trail descends into a depression. Topping a slight rise, it then descends to the southeast shore of Moraine Lake, a small lake in a rugged setting. Camping in the Moraine Lake area is at designated sites only, which are marked with a small post. Most of the sites are located north and east of the lake. Campfires are not allowed.

Beyond the lake, the trail turns east and southeast, following the drainage of Goose Creek in a moderately steep descent. The sound of Fall Creek can be heard well before it is reached; it is a large stream, draining Green Lake, the largest lake on the hike. At the junction with the Green Lakes Trail, turn left (north). There is plentiful camping in the next 0.2 mile, and this forested valley floor is more sheltered than Moraine Lake if bad weather threatens. The trail then leaves the creekside and climbs steeply for about 1 mile. It rejoins the creek at the foot of another impressive lava flow, then levels out into a narrow meadow. At the north end of the meadow, a trail goes left, around the west side of the lakes, and the Broken Top Trail comes in from the right a few yards away. Turn right, then left at this confusing junction, staying on the main Green Lakes Trail, which immediately skirts a small lake on the west. When the largest lake comes into view, be sure to stay to the right; the main trail does not descend to the lake edge, but instead climbs slightly to avoid the boggy, fragile terrain. Camping at the popular Green Lakes is restricted to designated sites only, and campfires are not allowed.

After skirting the main lake on the east, the trail passes a smaller lake on the west, then starts to climb up a ridge. In about 0.9 mile, the trail crosses a broad, open pass at 7,000 feet, the highest point on the hike. It then descends to the northeast into the forest. About 3 miles from Green Lakes, the trail drops into Park Meadow, a beautiful expanse of grass with superb views of the north side of Broken Top. There are several good campsites in the isolated stands of trees in the meadow, and water in Park Creek.

At the north edge of the meadow, turn left on the Pole Creek Trail, which descends gradually to the north though the lodgepole pine forest. It passes between two small lakes, then descends to cross the South Fork of Squaw Creek. This broad, flat valley offers numerous campsites in the open forest. The trail wanders north, crossing the North Fork of Squaw Creek. At Soap Creek, a sign points out the trail to Chambers Lakes, left; continue straight ahead on the Pole Creek Trail. This is the last late-season water source until Alder Creek, about 4.3 miles farther. In another 0.6 mile, turn left at a marked junction and head northwest. This trail climbs gradually for several miles, then starts to descend as it passes several small cinder meadows. The trail crosses Alder Creek, and there is limited camping north of the creek and trail.

Two miles beyond Alder Creek, turn left (west) on the Scott Trail. It climbs about 800 feet to Scott Pass, meeting the PCST where we left it at the east side of South Matthieu Lake. Follow the PCST around the north side of the lake, then stay with it at the junction with the Matthieu Lake Trail. The PCST continues north, staying high and contouring rather than descending into the forest. It provides some great views of the lava fields to the west and north. After about 0.4 mile, the trail enters the forest and eventually descends. The Matthieu Lake Trail joins from the right; stay on the PCST another 0.6 mile, then turn right on the Lava Camp Trail and walk the last 0.2 mile to the trailhead.

38 PROXY FALLS

General description:	A day hike to two waterfalls in the Three Sisters Wilderness.
Location:	About 13 miles east of McKenzie Bridge.
Maps:	Linton Lake USGS; Three Sisters Wilderness Geo-Graphics; Willamette National Forest.
Difficulty:	Easy.
Length:	1-mile loop.
Elevation:	3,100 to 3,160 feet.
Best season:	Summer and fall.
Permit:	Registration required at trailhead.
For more information:	McKenzie Ranger District, Willamette National Forest.

Key points:
    0.0 Trailhead.
    0.4 Right to Lower Proxy Falls.
    0.5 Lower Proxy Falls
    0.6 Right to Upper Proxy Falls.
    0.8 Upper Proxy Falls.
    1.0 Trailhead.

PROXY FALLS • LINTON LAKE TRAIL

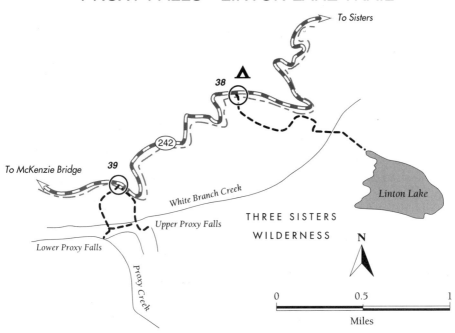

Finding the trailhead: From McKenzie Bridge, drive east about 4 miles on Oregon Highway 126, then turn right (east) on Oregon Highway 242. Continue 9 miles to the marked trailhead.

The hike: The trail starts on the south side of the highway and crosses an open, sunny ridge of boulders before descending slightly. Follow the signs to Lower Proxy Falls. After viewing the lower falls, again turn right on the main trail to reach Upper Proxy Falls. The falls, a steep cascade, plummets into a pool that drains underground except at high water.

Back at the fork in the trails, go right again to return to the trailhead.

39 *LINTON LAKE TRAIL*

General description:	A day hike to Linton Lake in the Three Sisters Wilderness.
Location:	About 14 miles east of McKenzie Bridge.
Maps:	Linton Lake USGS; Mount Washington Wilderness Geo-Graphics; Willamette National Forest.
Difficulty:	Easy.
Length:	2.8 miles round-trip.

Elevation:	3,500 to 3,700 feet.
Best season:	Summer and fall.
Permit:	Required for day and overnight hikes; self issue at trailhead.
For more information:	McKenzie Ranger District, Willamette National Forest.

Key points:
- 0.0 Trailhead.
- 0.7 High point of trail.
- 1.4 Linton Lake.

Finding the trailhead: From McKenzie Bridge, drive east about 4 miles on Oregon Highway 126, then turn right (east) on Oregon Highway 242. Continue 10 miles to the marked trailhead at Alder Springs Campground.

The hike: The hike follows the Linton Lake Trail through Douglas-fir forest, crossing White Branch Creek and then a low ridge. As you near the lake, you'll hear the unmistakable sound of Linton Falls, which is above the lake to the east. The lake itself is scenic, and the pleasant walk through the quiet forest is more than worthwhile.

40 *CASTLE ROCK*

General description:	A day hike to a scenic summit overlooking the glacially carved McKenzie River Valley.
Location:	About 11 miles south of Blue River.
Maps:	McKenzie Bridge USGS; Willamette National Forest.
Difficulty:	Moderate.
Length:	2 miles round-trip.
Elevation:	2,800 to 3,608 feet.
Best season:	Summer and fall.
Permit:	None.
For more information:	Blue River and McKenzie ranger districts, Willamette National Forest.

Key points:
- 0.0 Trailhead and junction; go right.
- 1.0 Castle Rock.

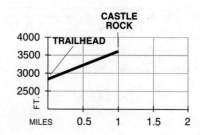

Upper McKenzie River Valley from Castle Rock.

Finding the trailhead: From Blue River, drive about 5 miles east on Oregon Highway 126, then turn south on paved Forest Road 19, marked for Cougar Reservoir. Go about 0.4 mile, then straight onto Forest Road 410, marked for Cougar Dam Powerhouse. After 0.2 mile, turn left (east) onto paved Forest Road 2639. Go 0.6 mile, then turn right (south) onto gravel Forest Road 480. Follow this road about 5 miles to its end at a small parking area.

The hike: Walk just a few yards up the trail from the trailhead, then turn right (west) on the marked trail for Castle Rock. A few short switchbacks lead up through dense Douglas-fir forest. The trail then climbs around the southwest slopes before switching back again to emerge on the grassy summit meadow. The old lookout site at the northwest end of the summit ridge has the best view west, down the McKenzie River Valley, while a viewpoint a few yards east has the best view up the valley toward Mount Washington and the Three Sisters. From either viewpoint, the classic U-shape of the McKenzie Valley is readily apparent. Stream channels are normally U-shaped, while valley sides are V-shaped. But this valley was carved by a huge stream, a river of ice flowing down from the high Cascades.

CASTLE ROCK

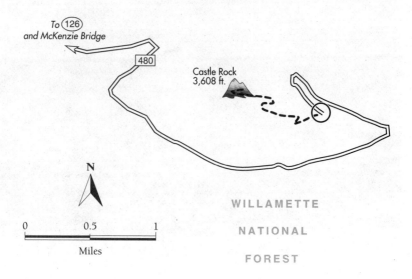

---

41 OLALLIE TRAIL

General description:	A day hike to a viewpoint overlooking the Three Sisters Wilderness.
Location:	About 22 miles south of Blue River.
Maps:	French Mountain USGS; Three Sisters Wilderness Geo-Graphics; Willamette National Forest.
Difficulty:	Moderate.
Length:	4.8 miles round-trip.
Elevation:	4,540 to 5,200 feet.
Best season:	Summer and fall.
Permit:	None.
For more information:	McKenzie and Blue River ranger districts, Willamette National Forest.

See Map on Page 121

Key points:

0.0   Trailhead.
1.1   Saddle and end of climb.
1.5   Potholes junction; stay left.
2.3   Three Sisters view.

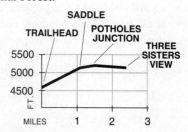

Finding the trailhead: From Blue River, drive about 5 miles east on Oregon Highway 126, then turn south on paved Forest Road 19, marked for

Old Forest Service phone line insulator.

Cougar Reservoir. After about 0.4 mile, turn right to stay on FR 19. Continue 3.2 miles, then turn left (east) on paved Forest Road 1993 and cross the dam. The road remains paved until it leaves the lake, then it becomes gravel. Continue to Pat's Saddle trailhead, on the right, about 14 miles from the dam.

The hike: From the trailhead, cross FR 1993 and start on the marked Olallie Trail. The trail heads up the slope through a forest with some large Douglas-fir. It switches back left, then right, then left again before reaching a saddle and leveling off. As it contours along the slopes of English Mountain, watch for old, white, donut-shaped insulators wired to the trees about ten to fifteen feet above the ground.

These were installed by the Forest Service to support a single wire phone line. The phone wire was strung through the donut, which was actually two pieces wired together, and looped from tree to tree. Since the wire wasn't attached to the insulator, it was free to move. This was a major advantage in the forest, where trees commonly fell across the line. There was enough slack in the wire so that it sagged to the ground rather than breaking. Of course, that shorted out the phone circuit, so the deadfall did have to be removed. Often it was the lookout's job to follow the line and remove any fallen trees. The phone lines connected fire lookouts, guard stations, dispatchers, and ranger stations, and different rings were used to alert the called party. In effect, it was one big party line. After hours, a lively round-table conversation was the norm, as people in widely spaced, lonely outposts would get caught up on unofficial business. After World War II radio supplanted the phone system.

The trail reaches a marked intersection with the spur trail to Potholes Camp; stay left. After about another 0.8 mile, the trail reaches an open talus slope below Lamb Butte with a picture-postcard view of the Three Sisters. This makes a good ending for the hike.

42 OLALLIE MOUNTAIN

General description:	A day hike to a historic fire lookout in the Three Sisters Wilderness. The abandoned lookout features a 360-degree view of the western Cascades.
Location:	About 22 miles south of Blue River.
Maps:	French Mountain USGS; Three Sisters Wilderness Geo-Graphics; Willamette National Forest.
Difficulty:	Moderate.
Length:	6.8 miles round-trip.
Elevation:	4,540 to 5,680 feet.
Best season:	Summer and fall.
Permit:	Required for day and overnight hikes; self issue at trailhead.

OLALLIE TRAIL • OLALLIE MOUNTAIN

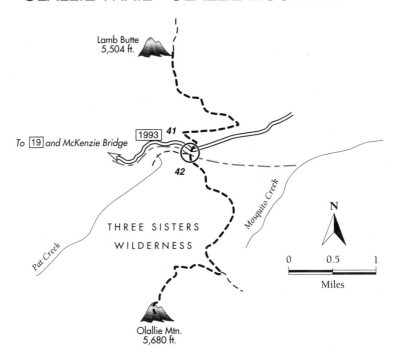

For more information: McKenzie and Blue River ranger districts, Willamette National Forest.

Finding the trailhead: Follow the directions for Hike 41

Key points:
0.0   Trailhead.
2.0   Olallie Mountain Trail; turn right.
3.4   Olallie Mountain lookout.

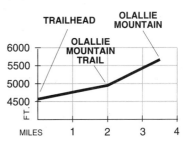

The hike: From the Pat Saddle trailhead, take the Olallie Meadows Trail south along the gentle ridge. The trail soon turns southeast and contours through Douglas-fir and grand fir forest. In less than 1 mile, the mountainside becomes much steeper, but the trail climbs only gently. Finally, as if it suddenly remembers that it's headed for a higher saddle, it starts to climb gradually.

Walk through the broad saddle; the trail starts to descend slightly before you reach a marked junction. Here, turn right on the Olallie Mountain Trail. This little-used trail climbs at a moderate rate through a forest now dominated by subalpine fir and mountain hemlock. It climbs steeply through a couple of

121

The Three Sisters from Olallie Mountain.

meadows, then levels out again before attacking the summit ridge. A couple of switchbacks on the west side of the mountain lead to the summit.

The old lookout building is still intact on the south end of the ridge, but is no longer in use. The lookout has a sweeping view. The high Cascades are visible from Mount Hood to Diamond Peak, and the mountain is a front row seat for the Three Sisters to the east. One of the most impressive features of the view is the sweep of unbroken forest from the base of the mountain to the Three Sisters timberline. The view to the west, down the forested length of French Pete Creek, is equally impressive. This mountaintop gives one a good feel for the appearance of the Cascades before the advent of large-scale clearcut logging.

43 FRENCH PETE CREEK

General description:	A day hike through old-growth forest in the Three Sisters Wilderness.
Location:	About 10 miles south of McKenzie Bridge.
Maps:	Cougar Reservoir USGS; Three Sisters Wilderness Geo-Graphics; Willamette National Forest.
Difficulty:	Easy.
Length:	3.2 miles round-trip.
Elevation:	1,800 to 2,200 feet.
Best season:	Year-round.
Permit:	Required for day and overnight hikes; self issue at trailhead.
For more information:	Blue River Ranger District, Willamette National Forest.

Key points:
0.0   Trailhead.
1.6   Bridge crossing.

Finding the trailhead: From Blue River, drive about 5 miles east on Oregon Highway 126, then turn south on Forest Road 19. After 0.4 mile, turn right again to remain on FR 19. Continue about 11 miles to the French Pete trailhead, on the left (east) side of the road.

The hike: The French Pete Trail follows French Pete Creek into a valley made famous by the conservation battle fought over it in the 1970s. Plans were being made to log the valley, but many felt it should be preserved. French Pete become symbolic of the battle to protect more than "rock and ice" wilderness. Many felt that intact lowland forest should be added to the protected areas. In the end, French Pete Creek's entire watershed become part of the Three Sisters Wilderness.

This hike follows the trail 1.6 miles to a bridge made from a single large log. The first mile is especially impressive for the massive Douglas-fir trees.

Old-growth Douglas-fir along the French Pete Creek Trail.

FRENCH PETE CREEK • REBEL CREEK

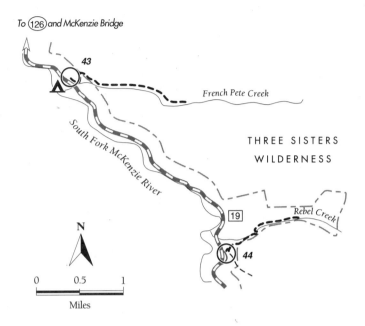

44 *REBEL CREEK*

General description:	A day hike through an old-growth Douglas-fir forest in the Three Sisters Wilderness.
Location:	About 12 miles south of McKenzie Bridge.
Maps:	Cougar Reservoir USGS; Three Sisters Wilderness Geo-Graphics; Willamette National Forest.
Difficulty:	Easy.
Length:	2.2 miles round-trip.
Elevation:	2,100 to 2,400 feet.
Best season:	Year-round.
Permit:	Required for day and overnight hikes; self issue at trailhead.
For more information:	Blue River Ranger District, Willamette National Forest.

Key points:
    0.0   Trailhead.
    0.6   First bridge crossing.
    1.1   Second bridge crossing.

Old-growth Douglas-fir, Rebel Creek.

Finding the trailhead: From Blue River, drive about 5 miles east on Oregon Highway 126, then turn south on Forest Road 19. After 0.4 mile, turn right again to remain on FR 19. Continue about 14 miles to the Rebel Creek trailhead, on the left (east) side of the road.

The hike: From the trailhead bulletin board, walk a few yards up the trail, then turn left (northeast) on the marked Rebel Creek Trail. The trail climbs up a bit, then contours through a relatively young section of forest for about 0.5 mile. It drops down to the creek and crosses it on a single log bridge. Now the trail passes through superb old-growth forest; watch for an especially large Douglas-fir on the left side of the trail. Fire scars on this tree and others show that they are survivors of a forest fire (possibly more than one). Douglas-fir evolved to accommodate fire. Its thick, corky bark protects the tree from all but high intensity crown fires.

The pleasant walk through the towering cathedral of trees continues as the trail makes its way along the north bank. At 1.1 miles, it comes to a second bridge crossing, which is the end of our hike. It is possible to make this easy hike into a strenuous loop by hiking up to Rebel Rock and returning via the Rebel Rock Trail.

45   ERMA BELL LAKES

General description:	A day hike or overnight backpack to a series of scenic lakes in the Three Sisters Wilderness.
Location:	About 31 miles south of McKenzie Bridge.
Maps:	Waldo Mountain USGS; Three Sisters Wilderness Geo-Graphics; Willamette National Forest.
Difficulty:	Moderate.
Length:	8-mile loop (including a 0.6 mile out-and-back section at the start).
Elevation:	4,500 to 5,120 feet.
Best season:	Summer and fall.
Permit:	Required for day and overnight hikes; self issue at trailhead.
For more information:	Oakridge Ranger District, Willamette National Forest.

Key points:

0.0	Trailhead.
0.6	Otter Lake Junction; go right.
1.7	Lower Erma Bell Lake.
2.1	Middle Erma Bell Lake.
2.7	Upper Erma Bell Lake.
3.3	Taylor Burn junction; turn left.
4.0	Williams Lake Trail junction; turn left.
4.4	Williams Lake.

6.6   Irish Mountain Trail junction at Otter Lake; go left.

7.4   Complete the loop at Erma Bell Trail junction; turn right.

8.0   Trailhead.

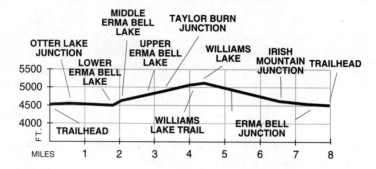

Finding the trailhead: From McKenzie Bridge, drive 27 miles south on paved Forest Road 19, then turn left onto gravel Forest Road 1957, which is marked for Skookum trailhead and campground. Continue 3.7 miles to the end of the road.

The hike: The Erma Bell Lakes Trail crosses a bridge, then contours south along a steep slope forested with Douglas-fir and grand fir. The portion of the trail leading to Lower Erma Bell Lake is almost completely level, and is obstacle free. It has been developed for wheelchair use, though this would probably still be an arduous trip. A trail, marked for Otter Lake, branches left and will be our return trail. Staying right, continue on the Erma Bell Lakes Trail. As the trail nears Lower Erma Bell Lake. Mountain hemlock becomes much more common. The lake is rockbound and very scenic. Note that camping is restricted to designated sites at all three Erma Bell lakes and at Otter Lake.

The trail skirts the west shore of the lake, then climbs a short distance to Middle Erma Bell Lake. Just before reaching the middle lake, an unmarked turnoff goes left to the exit stream and a nice little waterfall. The main trail skirts the west shore of the middle lake, then climbs gently to reach Upper Erma Bell Lake. An unmarked trail goes right, down to the upper lake. The upper lake is a good destination for those who would like to make this an easy hike.

The Erma Bell Lakes Trail now turns southeast and climbs onto a ridge with a single switchback. Western white pine becomes common in the forest, and lodgepole pine makes an appearance on this warmer, drier ridge. The trail then meets a trail to Taylor Burn trailhead at a marked junction. Turn left and follow the trail as it climbs gently for 0.7 mile to another trail junction. Subalpine fir and Engelmann spruce make an appearance along this section. Here, turn left (south) onto the little-used Williams Lake Trail, which you'll use to make the hike into a loop.

ERMA BELL LAKES

The trail passes Williams Lake, which is small and shallow, then reaches the high point of the hike just beyond the outlet. Watch for outcrops of rock with glacial striations, scratches that tell the direction of ice movement. The forest becomes more alpine in character, with more lodgepole pine and subalpine fir. The trail passes though several nice meadows about 1 mile north of Williams Lake. It then swings to the west and descends to reach Otter Lake and a trail junction. Stay left here, and skirt Otter Lake on the west, then rejoin the Erma Bell Lakes Trail. Turn right (north) and hike back to the trailhead.

46 LITTLE THREE CREEK LAKE

General description:	A day hike to a small lake with an impressive backdrop formed by the Tam McArthur Rim.
Location:	About 15 miles south of Sisters.
Maps:	Broken Top USGS; Three Sisters Wilderness Geo-Graphics; Deschutes National Forest.
Difficulty:	Easy.
Length:	2.2 miles round-trip.
Elevation:	6,560 to 6,700 feet.
Best season:	Summer and fall.
Permit:	None.
For more information:	Sisters Ranger District, Deschutes National Forest.

Little Three Creek Lake below the Tam McArthur Rim.

Key points:
  0.0   Trailhead.
  0.1   First Three Creek Meadow Trail junction; turn left.
  0.7   Second Three Creek Meadow Trail junction; turn left again.
  1.1   Little Three Creek Lake.

Finding the trailhead: From Sisters, drive south on paved Forest Road 16, marked for Three Creek Lake. Stay on the main road after the pavement ends. Turn right on the marked road for Driftwood Campground, just as you reach Three Creek Lake. The trailhead is marked and is on the right just before the campground.

The hike: This easy trail meanders through lodgepole pine and mountain hemlock forest. Just after leaving the trailhead, a marked trail branches right to Three Creek Meadow. Stay left here. Just after crossing a stream, you'll reach a four-way junction. Turn left to stay on the Little Three Creek Lakes Trail. It now follows the outlet stream from the lake to reach a pair of nice meadows and then the lake itself. The view of the Tam McArthur Rim is close-up and imposing, as the rim seems to wrap itself around the lake.

LITTLE THREE CREEK LAKE
TAM McARTHUR RIM

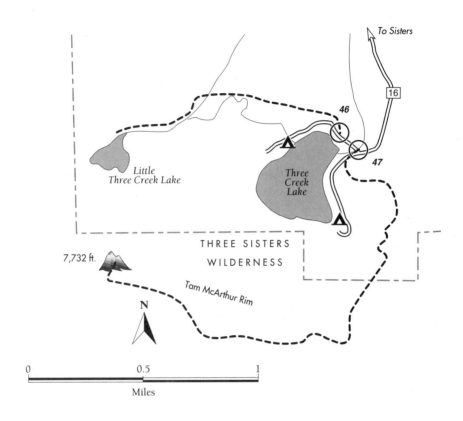

To Sisters

16

46

Little
Three Creek Lake

Three
Creek
Lake

47

THREE SISTERS

7,732 ft.

WILDERNESS

Tam McArthur Rim

N

| 0 | 0.5 | 1 |

Miles

47 *TAM McARTHUR RIM*

General description:	A day hike to a rugged overlook in the Three Sisters Wilderness.
Location:	About 15 miles south of Sisters.
Maps:	Broken Top, Tumalo Falls USGS; Three Sisters Wilderness Geo-Graphics; Deschutes National Forest.
Difficulty:	Moderate.
Length:	5.6 miles round-trip.
Elevation:	6,550 to 7,730 feet.
Best season:	Summer and fall.
Permit:	Required for day and overnight hikes; self issue at trailhead.
For more information:	Sisters Ranger District, Deschutes National Forest.

131

Key points:

0.0 Trailhead.
2.0 Plateau.
2.8 Tam McArthur Rim.

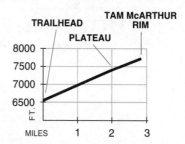

Finding the trailhead: From Sisters, drive south on paved Forest Road 16, marked for Three Creek Lake. Stay on the main road after the pavement ends. The trailhead is marked and is on the left just as you reach Three Creek Lake.

The hike: The Tam McArthur Rim is a popular hike for those staying at the nearby campgrounds. The trail starts climbing immediately, switching back south above the lake. It reaches a ridge crest, then follows it southwest, still climbing. When the trail reaches the eastern end of a broad plateau, the grade moderates. The north edge of this plateau forms the escarpment called the Tam McArthur Rim. Our goal is a promontory on the rim, which is clearly visible ahead. Follow the trail about 0.7 mile farther, then turn right at an unmarked fork to reach the promontory.

The plateau continues to slope up to the west, eventually merging with the east ridge of Broken Top. From the edge of the rim, the Three Creek Lake basin spreads out at our feet. To the west, the Three Sisters are spaced nicely along the Cascade crest. Mount Washington and Mount Jefferson are visible to the northwest, and to the south, the cone of Bachelor Butte is unmistakable.

Our high vantage point lies near timberline, and the small trees show evidence of their struggle with the harsh elements. The low, prostrate trees on the promontory are called krummholz. Here the wind is so strong and cold that trees grow behind protective boulders, or in places where the snow drifts in winter. Any attempt to grow above the protective rock or snowdrift fails, so in effect the tree is trained by the wind. A few yards to the north, conditions appear to be slightly better. Here, some trunks manage to stand above the snow drift level. These were able to grow fast enough during their first growing season to escape the worst of the abrasion from wind-blown snow. The limbs on the upper trunks of some of these trees grow in a single direction, away from the prevailing wind. These "flag trees" are unable to grow branches into the wind because the new growth is frost-killed.

132

Tam McArthur Rim.

General description:	A less-used trail that provides a day hike or overnight backpack along the slopes of Broken Top Mountain in the Three Sisters Wilderness. This hike remains near timberline with excellent views.
Location:	About 30 miles west of Bend.
Maps:	Broken Top USGS; Three Sisters Wilderness Geo-Graphics; Deschutes National Forest.
Difficulty:	Difficult.
Length:	11.4 miles round-trip, including a loop around the Green Lakes.
Elevation:	7,080 to 6,500 feet.
Best season:	Summer and fall.
Permit:	Required for day and overnight hikes; self issue at trailhead.
For more information:	Bend-Fort Rock Ranger District, Deschutes National Forest.

Key points:

- 0.0 Trailhead.
- 0.6 Crater Creek Ditch.
- 1.8 Continue straight at the Soda Creek Trail junction.
- 4.5 Green Lakes Trail; go left, then immediately right on the unnamed trail along the west side of Green Lake.
- 6.1 Turn right on the Green Lakes Trail.
- 6.9 Turn left on the Broken Top Trail.
- 11.4 Trailhead.

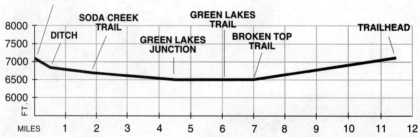

Finding the trailhead: From Bend, drive west about 26 miles on Oregon Highway 46, then turn right at the sign for Todd Lake. The road is closed in winter beyond the Todd Lake trailhead. Here the road (Forest Road 370) becomes much rougher and starts to climb. A high-clearance vehicle is recommended. Continue 4.2 miles from the highway, then turn left (northwest) onto Forest Road 380. Follow this road 1.4 miles to its end at the trailhead.

Green Lakes.

The hike: If you plan to do this hike as an overnight, you may wish to consider camping at one of the many campsites along the trail, rather than at Green Lakes. The lakes area is heavily used; the Forest Service restricts camping to designated sites, and campfires are not allowed. Pick up a map of the restricted area at the trailhead.

The trail starts out on an old road, then branches left when just out of sight of the trailhead. It then works its way down a gentle slope through a pleasant, open forest of timberline trees, such as subalpine fir. It descends in a final switchback and, at 0.6 mile, crosses the Crater Creek Ditch, an irrigation diversion project. The enjoyable next section crosses an open basin with views of the south slopes of Broken Top and the Crook Glacier. At the far side of this basin, the trail climbs slightly and starts to traverse the sleeper slopes of Cayuse Crater, a prominent cinder cone on the southwest ridge of Broken Top. Here, the Soda Creek Trail joins from the left at a marked junction. The main trail swings around the reddish slopes of Cayuse Crater through scattered trees, then crosses another open basin with excellent views to the south and southwest. The trail rounds another spur of Broken Top, and South Sister begins to dominate the view ahead. Notice the massive lava flow spilling down its southeast slopes. After another mile, the trail begins to descend toward the Green Lakes. It ends at the junction with the Green Lakes Trail.

The hike can end here if you are satisfied with a view of Green Lakes (this would make the hike 9 miles round-trip). However, it's worth walking down to the main Green Lake and around it. To do this, turn left at this marked junction, then, in 50 feet, turn right on the unnamed trail that heads around the west side of the lakes. A jagged lava flow forms the west side of the valley, and the trail heads north across the outwash plain at the foot of the lava.

After crossing a small stream, the outwash plain becomes increasingly wet, and the trail fades away. Veer left toward the talus slope and cross the next stream right at the base of the slope. Looking east from this point, the views of Broken Top are superb. Now turn right (northwest) and walk around the north side of the lake, avoiding the wet ground near the shore. As you near the slopes on the east side of the lake, aim for the lakeshore. The inlet stream is small, at least in late season, and easy to cross. Climb the slope about 200 feet to reach the Green Lakes Trail, then turn right. From this area along the east side of the Green Lakes you will be treated to some of the finest views of the east slopes of South Sister. Follow the trail north along the east shore of the main lake, and then along the east shore of the small southern lake, to rejoin the Broken Top Trail. Now turn left (east) to return to the trailhead.

BROKEN TOP TRAIL
TODD LAKE TRAIL
FALL CREEK

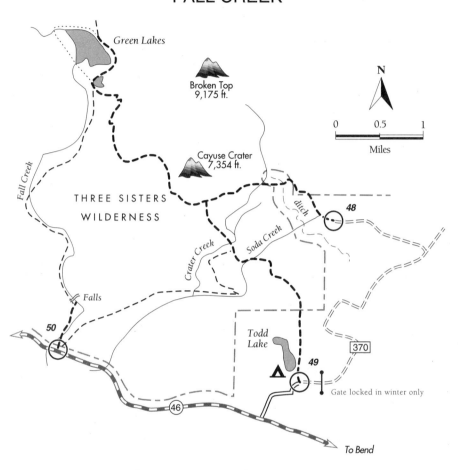

49 *TODD LAKE TRAIL*

General description:	A day hike or overnight backpack to Green Lakes in the Three Sisters Wilderness. The trail winds through alpine meadows with views of Broken Top Mountain.
Location:	About 28 miles west of Bend.
Maps:	Broken Top USGS; Three Sisters Wilderness Geo-Graphics; Deschutes National Forest.
Difficulty:	Difficult.
Length:	11.8 miles round-trip.

Elevation:	6,100 to 6,760 feet.
Best season:	Summer and fall.
Permit:	Required for day and overnight hikes; self issue at trailhead
For more information:	Bend-Fort Rock Ranger District, Deschutes National Forest.

Key points:
- 0.0   Trailhead.
- 0.1   Go right on the Todd Lake Trail.
- 2.4   Soda Creek Trail on left; continue straight.
- 3.2   Broken Top Trail.
- 5.9   Green Lakes.

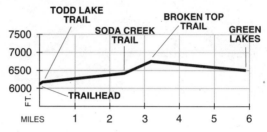

Finding the trailhead: From Bend, drive west about 25 miles on the Cascade Lakes Highway (Oregon Highway 46), then turn right at the sign for Todd Lake. Go about 0.5 mile on the gravel road and park at the Todd Lake trailhead.

The hike: This is a good alternative route to the Broken Top Trail and Green Lakes for those without the high-clearance vehicle recommended to reach the Broken Top trailhead.

Walk up the first short section of trail, an old road, to the wilderness registration sign and the sign marking the start of the Todd Lake Trail. It's a right turn. The trail immediately starts climbing the forested slope east of the lake. There are occasional glimpses of the lake through the trees. After about 1 mile the trail levels off and passes through some small meadows, descending slightly. There are good views of Broken Top and South Sister. In another mile, the trail descends left to cross Soda Creek. After this point, the view opens up as the trail enters the southwest portion of the broad basin south of Broken Top.

After crossing a sandy flat, the Soda Creek Trail comes in from the left at a marked junction; go straight ahead. The trail crosses Crater Creek and starts to climb toward Cayuse Crater, the red cinder cone on the south ridge of Broken Top. Rounding a low hill, the trail ends at the junction with the Broken Top Trail.

Turn left and walk about 2.7 miles to Green Lakes. It is also possible to explore the basin to the right. For details on the Broken Top Trail, as well as camping at Green Lakes, see Hike 48.

The meadows and isolated stands of trees in the Crater Creek drainage and the Green Lakes area are good examples of alpine scenery. Notice how

Alpine meadow and tree islands along the Todd Lake Trail.

the trees tend to form clumps or small groups in the higher areas. These tree islands form around a single original tree, usually a mountain hemlock or whitebark pine that was lucky enough to find a hospitable enough spot to become established. As other trees take advantage of the protection of the pioneer tree, the tree island expands. The trees not only form a windbreak but also absorb solar heat, forming a warmer microclimate than the surrounding meadows. Tree islands tend to form on rises or hummocks where the snow is less deep and melts earlier. In cool, windy weather the tree islands are often surprisingly cozy places for a lunch stop or campsite. Wildlife finds the tree islands to be hospitable refuges as well.

50   FALL CREEK

General description:	A short day hike to an excellent waterfall in the Three Sisters Wilderness.
Location:	About 28 miles west of Bend.
Maps:	Broken Top USGS; Three Sisters Wilderness Geo-Graphics; Deschutes National Forest.
Difficulty:	Easy.
Length:	1.2 miles round-trip.
Elevation:	5,440 to 5,560 feet.
Best season:	Summer and fall.
Permit:	Required for day and overnight hikes; self issue at trailhead.
For more information:	Bend-Fort Rock Ranger District, Deschutes National Forest.

See Map on Page 137

Key points:
    0.0   Trailhead.
    0.6   Fall Creek falls.

Finding the trailhead: From Bend, drive west on the Cascade Lakes Highway (Oregon Highway 46) about 28 miles, and turn right (north) at the Green Lakes trailhead.

The hike: This hike goes a short distance up the Green Lakes Trail to a fine waterfall on Fall Creek. After leaving the parking area, the trail crosses the creek on a bridge then ascends the slope west of the creek. After about 0.6 mile, the roar of the creek seems to fade as the trail starts to climb away from it. You will see an unmarked trail turning off to the right. Follow the trail downstream about 100 feet to a point overlooking the falls. The trail continues to the base of the falls. Although the height of the falls is only about 20 feet, the water from the creek is spread out nicely at the lip, making the fall about 40 feet wide at low water.

This trail is the most popular route to Green Lakes and, accordingly, is heavily used. For lesser used trails, see Hikes 48 and 49.

The falls, Fall Creek.

General description:	A day hike with great views of South Sister, in the Three Sisters Wilderness.
Location:	About 28 miles west of Bend.
Maps:	South Sister USGS; Three Sisters Wilderness Geo-Graphics; Deschutes National Forest.
Difficulty:	Moderate.
Length:	5-mile loop.
Elevation:	5,450 to 6,650 feet.
Best season:	Summer and fall.
Permit:	Required for day and overnight hikes; self issue at trailhead.
For more information:	Bend-Fort Rock Ranger District, Deschutes National Forest.

Key points:

0.0   Trailhead at Devils Lake.
0.8   Elk Lake Trail; stay right.
1.6   Sisters Mirror Lake Trail goes left; stay right, toward Moraine Lake.
2.0   Wickiup Plain Trail joins from left; stay right again.
3.2   Turn right on the South Sister Climbers Trail.
4.8   Trailhead at Devils Lake.

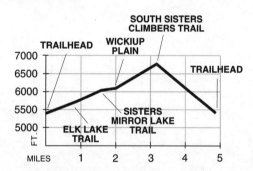

Finding the trailhead: From Bend, drive west on the Cascade Lakes Highway (Oregon Highway 46) about 29 miles to the marked South Sister-Sisters Mirror Lake trailhead at Devils Lake.

The hike: There is no water along this hike in late summer; be sure to carry some. Start the loop by hiking the Sisters Mirror Lake Trail from the south end of the parking area. The trail goes under the highway, then climbs gradually west. The sound of Tyee Creek just to the north soon ends; this source of Devils Lake is fed by springs only 0.5 mile away. Just after the sound of the creek ends, you'll come to the junction with the Elk Lake Trail; stay right, toward Wickiup Plain.

The trail turns a little more to the northwest and climbs more steeply, along the base of steep-sided Kaleetan Butte. As the trail levels out, you meet another junction. Turn right on the Moraine Lake Trail, which soon enters the stark expanse of Wickiup Plain, a cinder desert. You reach another trail junction in about 0.5 mile; again stay right on the Moraine Lake Trail. The trail enters the forest again and climbs for about 0.3 mile before emerging on a treeless plain again. There are great views of South Sister. Rock Mesa, a massive flow of obsidian-rich lava, is visible to the north. It's an easy but optional 0.5-mile stroll over to the base of the lava flow, and well worth the side trip. This adds 1 mile to the hike.

Follow the main trail as it enters the forest again for another stretch of serious climbing. When the trail emerges from the woods onto a flat, open plateau, the reward is a view of Broken Top. Shortly, you'll reach the junction with the South Sister Climbers Trail. Turn right here, leaving the Moraine Lake Trail behind. The Climbers Trail immediately plunges down the steep nameless ravine between Kaleetan Butte and Devils Hill. The initial grade soon moderates, but the trail still descends rapidly. As the grade moderates, the pleasant sound of spring-fed Hell Creek is heard. Soon the trail crosses the highway then emerges on the north side of the Devils Lake parking lot.

South Sister.

WICKIUP PLAIN
SISTERS MIRROR LAKE

Rock Mesa

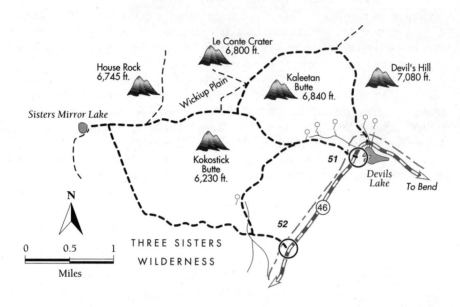

Le Conte Crater
6,800 ft.

House Rock
6,745 ft.

Wickiup Plain

Kaleetan
Butte
6,840 ft.

Devil's Hill
7,080 ft.

Sisters Mirror Lake

Kokostick
Butte
6,230 ft.

51

Devils
Lake

To Bend

52

46

N

0   0.5   1

Miles

THREE SISTERS
WILDERNESS

52   SISTERS MIRROR LAKE

General description:	A day hike to a group of small lakes in the Three Sisters Wilderness. This hike features numerous small lava flows.
Location:	About 30 miles west of Bend.
Maps:	South Sister USGS; Three Sisters Wilderness Geo-Graphics; Deschutes National Forest.
Difficulty:	Moderate.
Length:	8.5-mile loop.
Elevation:	5,400 to 6,040 feet.
Best season:	Summer and fall.
Permit:	Required for day and overnight hikes; self issue at trailhead.
For more information:	Bend-Fort Rock Ranger District, Deschutes National Forest.

Key points:
0.0   Trailhead.
0.4   Go straight ahead on the Sisters Mirror Lakes Trail.
3.2   Turn left on the Pacific Crest National Scenic Trail (PCST).

3.6   Sisters Mirror Lake.
4.0   Go straight ahead on the PCST.
4.5   The PCST turns left; continue straight, toward Moraine Lake.
5.5   The Wickiup Plain trail joins from the left; continue straight;
5.7   Turn right toward Devils Lake.
6.5   Turn right onto the Elk Lake Trail.
8.1   Turn left, rejoining the Sisters Mirror Lake Trail.
8.5   Trailhead.

Finding the trailhead: From Bend, go west on the Cascades Lakes Highway (Oregon Highway 46) about 30 miles to the marked trailhead for Sisters Mirror Lakes on the right (west).

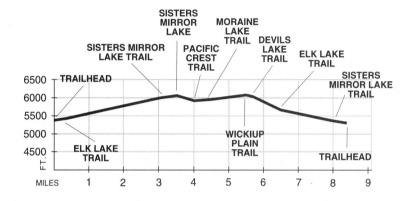

Sisters Mirror Lake.

The hike: The Sisters Mirror Lakes Trail starts by wandering west through hummocky ground left by lava flows. Then it drops into Sink Creek and meets the Elk Lake Trail, which crosses left to right. Continue straight ahead. At first, the trail climbs along a tributary of Sink Creek, but soon veers away and starts climbing a little more steeply along the south base of Kokostick Butte. After passing a small pond, the trail traverses a region of small lava flows and meadows. Several detours are necessary for the trail to avoid having to cross the rough surface of a flow. Another small lake is on its right, and shortly the trail enters a small meadow with a view of Koosah Mountain to the left (west).

After another mile, you reach a trail junction. After a short side trip to Sisters Mirror Lake, you'll be proceeding on the PCST northbound, which is a right (east) turn as you first approach this junction. For now, turn left on the PCST (southbound) and follow it about 0.4 mile to Sisters Mirror Lake. (There is another trail junction along the way—stay on the marked PCST.) Sisters Mirror Lake is a shallow one, set in a large meadow. By walking around the southwest side of the lake, you will see the summit of South Sister reflected in the lake, rising above the forested skyline of The House Rock in the foreground.

To continue the loop, follow the PCST east to the junction with the Mirror Lakes Trail, then continue east on the PCST. There are numerous trail junctions in the next 2 miles; turn right at all of them and you'll be on the correct trail. The trail spends a nice 0.5 mile threading through small meadows. The PCST goes left at a marked junction. Stay right, on the trail to Moraine Lake. After about 1 mile, another trail forks left toward Wickiup Plain. Again, stay right. Finally, in another 0.3 mile, turn right on the trail to Devils Lake trailhead. Follow this trail downhill about 1.1 miles, then turn right on the marked Elk Lake Trail. For a little more than 1 mile, this trail traverses dry forest, primarily lodgepole pine. Then it passes the source springs for Sink Creek, and the sound of flowing water is usually audible for the last 0.5 mile to the Mirror Lakes Trail. Turn left on the Mirror Lakes Trail and return to the trailhead, which is about 0.5 mile away.

53   CINDER HILL

General description:	A day hike to a scenic viewpoint overlooking East Lake and Newberry Crater in Newberry Crater National Monument.
Location:	About 40 miles south of Bend.
Maps:	East Lake USGS; Deschutes National Forest.
Difficulty:	Moderate.
Length:	5.8 miles round-trip.
Elevation:	6,400 to 7,420 feet.
Best season:	Summer and fall.
Permit:	None.
For more information:	Newberry Crater National Volcanic Monument.

Key points:
- 0.0   Trailhead at campsite 70.
- 0.1   Newberry Crater Trail, turn left.
- 1.7   Rim trail, go right.
- 2.9   Cinder Hill.

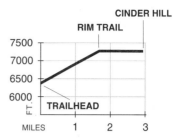

Finding the trailhead: From Bend, drive about 23 miles south on U.S. Highway 97, then turn left (east) at the sign for Newberry Crater and Paulina Lake. Continue 17 miles on this paved road, pass the East Lake Resort, and drive into Cinder Hill Campground. The trailhead is near campsite 70 at the far north end of the campground. Late in the season, the northern section of the campground will be closed, and you will have to park at the closure gate. Don't block the gate or any of the campsites.

The hike: The trail heads away from the campground and the lake, and almost immediately encounters a marked trail junction. Turn left (north) and follow the gently climbing Newberry Crater Trail. The first section of trail passes through thick lodgepole pine with many dead trees. This unattractive forest is soon left behind as the trail enters a canyon. Mountain hemlock appears and adds some alpine character to the forest. A switchback marks the start of steeper climbing near the head of the canyon, and soon more switchbacks lead to the crater rim.

Turn right (east) at the marked junction and follow the rim trail along the broad, nearly flat rim. Watch for mountain bikes, since the trail is very popular with riders. You'll notice a few whitebark pine mixed in with the lodgepole pine and mountain hemlock. The trail climbs slightly to reach the high point of the hike, then descends slightly to an open cinder slope. The expansive view to the east includes East Lake and part of Paulina Lake, as well as Paulina Mountain and, in the distance, Diamond Peak.

Newberry "Crater" is actually not a crater at all, but rather a caldera much like the more famous one at Crater Lake. After repeated eruptions emptied the central magma chamber under the caldera, it began to sink. As it sank, the walls of the caldera collapsed, widening the depression. Originally a single large lake flooded the floor of the caldera, but more recent eruptions in the center of the caldera have divided the lake into the present East Lake and Paulina Lake. The Newberry Volcano has erupted hundreds of times since its birth more than a half million years ago and now covers over 500 square miles. The most recent eruption was 1,300 years ago when the Big Obsidian Flow erupted from near the south rim of the caldera. Geothermal drilling shows that hot rocks are still found not far below the surface, suggesting that future eruptions are likely.

Whitebark pine, Cinder Hill.

CINDER HILL
PAULINA LAKE

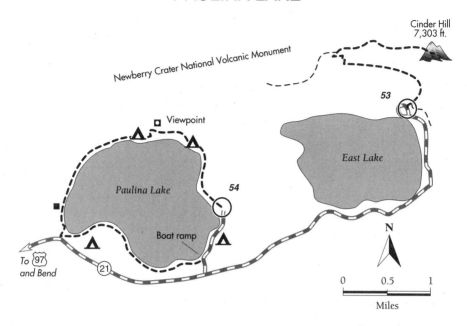

---

54   *PAULINA LAKE*

General description:	A nearly level day hike around beautiful Paulina Lake in Newberry National Volcanic Monument.
Location:	About 38 miles south of Bend.
Maps:	Paulina Lake, East Lake USGS; Deschutes National Forest.
Difficulty:	Moderate.
Length:	6.4-mile loop.
Elevation:	6,340 to 6,520 feet.
Best season:	Summer and fall.
Permit:	None.
For more information:	Newberry Crater National Volcanic Monument.

Key points:

0.0	Trailhead.
1.0	Warm Springs Campground.
1.5	Viewpoint.
1.9	North Cove Campground.
3.5	Paulina Lake Resort.
5.7	Boat ramp.
6.4	Trailhead.

Paulina Lake.

Finding the trailhead: From Bend, drive 23 miles south on U.S. Highway 97, then turn left (east) at the sign for Newberry Crater and Paulina Lake. Continue 14 miles on this paved road, then turn left (north) at the sign for Little Crater Campground. Drive about 0.9 mile to the north end of the campground and park at the trailhead. If the campground is closed, park at the entrance and walk through the campground.

The hike: The Paulina Lake Shoreline Trail starts off following the immediate shoreline, which is rocky and picturesque. The volcanic rocks form little alcoves and overhangs, which the abundant wildlife likes. The forest starts out with lodgepole pine dominating, but the true firs and mountain hemlock quickly mix in. Shortly you'll pass along the base of the Inter Lake Flow, a lava flow spanning the divide between Paulina and East lakes. After the flow, the shoreline becomes more gentle and even marshy in sections.

The trail passes Warm Springs Campground, a small, primitive campsite for boaters, then starts to climb away from the lake as it starts to round the north shore. At the top of this climb, the trail traverses a cinder slope about 200 feet above the lake. The open ponderosa pine stand allows great views of the lake from this vantage point. The trail now descends back to the lakeshore and passes a second boaters' campground, North Cove Campground, where there is a short section of cinder beach. The long section of trail along the west shore is especially scenic, because the trail is once again just above the rocky shoreline. The trail enters Paulina Lake Resort and becomes vague. Stay as close to the shoreline as possible past the dock. Then walk toward the entrance road and follow a short, unmarked section of trail to the outlet stream. Cross the creek on the road bridge, then pick up the trail again on the far side. The trail stays next to the shore through Paulina Lake Campground; if you lose it, walk the campground loop road until you see the trail again. After this, the trail rounds a point, then swings southeast along the lakeshore. It passes two groups of summer homes, then reaches the boat ramp on the Little Crater Campground road. Follow the road through the campground back to the trailhead.

ADDITIONAL TRAILS

Tidbits Mountain Trail starts from Forest Road 1509 north of Blue River and climbs to the top of Tidbits Mountain.

Frissel Trail starts from Forest Road 700 just north of McKenzie Bridge and climbs to the north rim of the McKenzie River Valley.

Scott Trail starts from Oregon Highway 242 west of McKenzie Pass and joins the Pacific Crest National Scenic Trail (PCST) south of Yapoah Crater.

Obsidian Way Trail starts from OR 242 and joins the PCST south of Obsidian Falls. A spur trail, the Glacier Way Trail, connects to the PCST at Glacier Creek. The Obsidian trailhead and Obsidian area are limited entry; a permit for day and overnight hikes must be picked up at the McKenzie Ranger Station in advance.

Substitute Point Trail starts from Forest Road 485 and climbs to the PCST; a spur trail climbs Substitute Point.

Trail 3520 starts from Forest Road 480 and connects to several trails, including the PCST, in the Linton Meadow area.

Separation Creek Trail connects the lower end of Trail 3520, via Separation Creek, to the Linton Meadow area.

Horse Lake Trail starts from Forest Road 2638 and traverses a long section of west side forest to reach the Horse Lake area. Numerous trails branch from this point, connecting to the PCST and the Elk Lake trailhead.

Nash Lake Trail connects the midpoint of the Horse Lake Trail to the Sisters Mirror Lake area.

Olallie Trail continues north past Taylor Castle, then meets Forest Road 1993. Several trails branch off, including Trail 3321, which ends at Forest Road 411 near Cougar Dam.

Lowder Mountain Trail starts from FR 1993 southwest of Blue River and climbs Lowder Mountain. A side trail goes to Yankee Mountain.

French Pete Creek Trail continues up French Pete Creek, then climbs up Pat Creek to Pat Creek Trailhead on FR 1993.

Rebel Creek Trail continues up Rebel Creek and connects with the Rebel Rock Trail, which makes a loop back to the Rebel Creek trailhead.

Chucksney Mountain Trail starts from Forest Road 19 south of Blue River and makes a loop over Chucksney Mountain.

Scott Trail (east) starts from the Scott's Pass trailhead on Forest Road 1026, west of Sisters, and climbs to Scott Pass from the east.

Pole Creek Trail starts from Forest Road 1524, southwest of Sisters, and climbs to the scenic Chambers Lakes area between Middle and South Sisters.

Park Meadow Trail starts from Forest Road 16 south of Sisters and goes to scenic Park Meadow.

Soda Creek Trail starts from the Fall Creek-Green Lakes trailhead on Oregon Highway 46 west of Bend and joins the Todd Lake Trail.

Tumalo Mountain Trail starts from OR 46 across from the Mount Bachelor Ski Area and climbs to the summit of Tumalo Mountain.

Pacific Crest National Scenic Trail continues south from Sisters Mirror Lake, following the crest for a few miles, then wandering west past numerous lakes in the Mink Lake area. It continues along the east slopes of Irish Mountain and leaves the Three Sisters Wilderness at the Irish Lake trailhead.

Elk Lake Trail continues south from the Sisters Mirror Lake Trail, paralleling OR 46, to end at the Elk Lake trailhead.

Elk Lake Trailhead on OR 46 near Elk Lake has three trails; the Elk Lake Trail mentioned above and two others that head west to the PCST and the Horse Lake area. Several loops are possible.

Six Lakes Trail starts from the Six Lakes trailhead on OR 46 south of Elk Lake. The trail goes past Blow and Doris lakes to meet the PCST and then continues on to the Mink Lake area.

Lucky Lake Trail starts from the Lucky Lake trailhead on OR 46 south of Elk Lake, passes Lucky Lake, then continues past Williamson Mountain and joins the Six Lakes Trail.

Cultus Lake Trail starts from Forest Road 100 on the east shore of Cultus Lake and runs northwest to join the PCST near Packsaddle Mountain.

Crater Rim Trail circles Newberry Crater in Newberry Crater National Volcanic Monument.

Peter Skene Ogden Trail starts from Oregon Highway 21 near Paulina Lake Resort and follows Paulina Creek to the west trailhead, also on OR 21.

Paulina Peak Trail starts from Forest Road 500 in Newberry Crater National Volcanic Monument and climbs to the summit of Paulina Peak.

WALDO LAKE

OVERVIEW

The Waldo Lake Wilderness is one of many wilderness areas established by the Oregon Wilderness Bill in 1984. The 37,162-acre wilderness borders the Waldo Lake Trail around the south, west, and north sides of Waldo Lake and covers much of the adjacent high country. Waldo Lake and hundreds of other smaller lakes were formed by the scouring and damming action of the glaciers that once covered the entire area. It is estimated that the ice cap in this area was more than 15,000 feet thick, forming an extensive ice field. Because of the high elevation and the lack of permanent inlet streams, Waldo Lake is exceptionally clear. The lake's outlet is at its north end, where the lake forms the headwaters of the Middle Fork of the Willamette River. However, at Klovdahl Bay, along the southwest shore, only a low ridge separates the lake from the depths of Black Creek. An attempt was actually made to exploit the hydropower potential, but it eventually failed, leaving the lake in its pristine condition.

55 KOCH MOUNTAIN TRAIL

General description:	A day hike or easy overnight backpack trip through a parklike alpine forest to the west shore of Waldo Lake in the Waldo Lake Wilderness.
Location:	About 26 miles east of Oakridge.
Maps:	Waldo Lake USGS; Waldo Lake Wilderness and Recreation Area, Willamette National Forest.
Difficulty:	Easy.
Length:	3.6 miles round-trip.
Elevation:	5,840 to 5,420 feet.
Best season:	Summer and fall.
Permit:	Permit required for day and overnight hikes; self issue at trailhead.
For more information:	Oakridge Ranger District, Willamette National Forest.

KOCH MOUNTAIN TRAIL
KLOVDAHL BAY

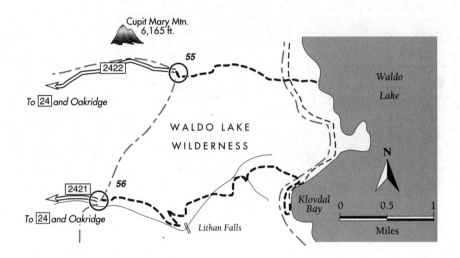

Key points:
- 0.0   Trailhead.
- 1.5   Waldo Lake Trail crossing; go straight.
- 1.8   Waldo Lake.

Finding the trailhead: From Oakridge on Oregon Highway 58, turn north at the sign for the post office, then drive east through the old downtown area. This road becomes Forest Road 24, the paved Salmon Creek Road. Continue until the pavement ends, 13.5 miles from OR 58, and the road becomes Forest Road 2421. Continue 0.5 mile, then turn left (north) on Forest Road 2422. Stay on this gravel road 12 miles to its end at the trailhead.

The hike: This hike is unusual for the west approaches to Waldo Lake in that it has a high-elevation trailhead. In fact, you will lose more than 400 feet hiking to the lake. The trail starts in a clearcut, then enters the wilderness area and starts to descend. Short steep sections of trail alternate with sections where the trail meanders through very pleasant, open-canopy pacific silver fir and mountain hemlock forest. After 1.5 miles of this enjoyable wandering, the trail descends to a junction. The Waldo Lake Trail crosses here, but go straight ahead (east). Your trail passes Green Lake, visible through the trees to the left, then reaches the shores of Waldo Lake. This vantage point in the middle of the long western shore gives you a feeling for just how large this unique alpine lake really is.

General description: A day hike or overnight backpack trip to Waldo Lake at the site of a historic water diversion tunnel in the Waldo Lake Wilderness.

Location: About 22 miles east of Oakridge.

Maps: Waldo Lake USGS; Waldo Lake Wilderness and Recreation Area, Willamette National Forest.

Difficulty: Difficult.

Length: 8.8 miles round-trip.

Elevation: 3,360 to 5,500 feet.

Best season: Summer and fall.

Permit: Permit required for day and overnight hikes; self issue at trailhead.

For more information: Oakridge Ranger District, Willamette National Forest.

Key points:

0.0   Trailhead.
1.3   Lithan Falls.
3.8   Waldo Lake Trail; turn right.
4.2   Klovdahl Trail; turn left.
4.4   Klovdahl Tunnel headgate.

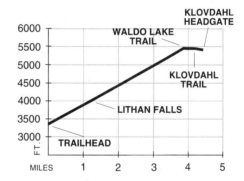

Finding the trailhead: From Oakridge on Oregon Highway 58, turn north at the sign for the post office, then drive east through the old downtown area. This road becomes Forest Road 24, the paved Salmon Creek Road. Continue until the pavement ends, 13.5 miles from OR 58, and the road becomes Forest Road 2421. Then continue 8.1 miles on gravel FR 2421 to its end at the trailhead for the Black Creek Trail.

The hike: Old-growth Douglas-fir provides a serene environment for the Black Creek Trail as it climbs along the slope north of the creek. The forest also contains western hemlock and western redcedar. After a little more than 1 mile the creek seems suddenly louder, and without any other warning the delightful cascade of Lithan Falls appears through the trees. This would make a good destination for those desiring an easy hike. The trail switches back to the left and climbs the north canyon wall.

At the top, the forest starts to take on a more alpine appearance, thanks to subalpine fir. A gentle section of trail follows where it crosses Nettie Creek. The trail resumes serious climbing when it encounters the steep glacial headwall of the canyon. It crosses through a burn that occurred during the severe 1996 fire season, then traverses a talus slope, offering a good view

Old headgate at Klovdahl Bay, Waldo Lake.

down Black Creek. The trail levels out as it follows pleasant Klovdahl Creek for a short distance, then crosses the creek and resumes the climb. Finally, the trail passes over a gentle ridge crest and drops a few feet to the shore of Waldo Lake and a junction with the Waldo Lake Trail. Turn right (south) and follow the trail about 0.4 mile. Now turn left (north) on the Klovdahl Trail, which follows the very edge of the lake. This spur trail ends at an old headgate structure, incongruously set into the shore of this wild lake.

Around the turn of the century, local development interests became aware of the possibilities the perched waters of Waldo Lake offered for irrigation and hydropower. In 1909 the Waldo Lake Irrigation and Power Company hired Simon Klovdahl, a civil engineer, to construct a channel through the low ridge separating Black Creek from the lake. Upon inspection, Klovdahl decided that the channel idea was impractical. Instead, a 500-foot tunnel was blasted through the rock. The water would be controlled by a headgate at the lake end of the tunnel.

The remote country and difficult travel made construction work difficult, but by 1914 the headgate was complete. The gate was capable of lowering the lake by 25 feet. A lack of markets for the water and power caused the company to fail by the early 1930s, a fortunate happening for the wilderness character of the lake. Studies have shown that the lake would take ten years to recover from a drawdown of twenty feet. Realizing the potential for an accidental loss of water from the lake, in 1960 the Forest Service hired divers to seal the gates with concrete. In 1987 a concrete plug was placed in the tunnel, downstream of the headgate, to fix a leak.

General description:	A day hike to a scenic, high peak overlooking Waldo Lake on the edge of the Waldo Lake Wilderness.
Location:	About 23 miles east of Oakridge.
Maps:	Waldo Lake USGS; Waldo Lake Wilderness and Recreation Area, Willamette National Forest.
Difficulty:	Moderate.
Length:	3 miles round-trip.
Elevation:	6,160 to 7,144 feet.
Best season:	Summer and fall.
Permit:	Permit required for day and overnight hikes; self issue at trailhead.
For more information:	Oakridge Ranger District, Willamette National Forest.

Key points:

0.0 Trailhead.
0.3 Trail junction; turn left.
1.5 Fuji Mountain.

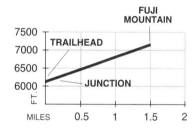

Finding the trailhead: From Oakridge, drive east about 13 miles on Oregon Highway 58, then turn left (north) on Forest Road 5883, a gravel road. Continue 10.4 miles and park at the trailhead for Fuji Mountain Trail.

The hike: The trail climbs gradually through a clearcut for several hundred yards, then veers right into the forest. Mountain hemlock and grand fir are the main trees forming the beautiful, parklike, high altitude forest. At a marked trail junction, turn left (west), staying on the Fuji Mountain Trail. The climb continues through the open forest; the trail keeps to an easy grade. Several switchbacks lead to the west shoulder of the mountain, where the forest becomes distinctly more timberline in character. The graceful spires of subalpine fir crowd among the mountain hemlocks. The summit, another former fire lookout site, is flat and open in all directions. In good weather you can see Cascade peaks from Mount Hood to Scott Peak. It's surprising the Forest Service closed the old lookout since it has such a good vantage point for spotting fires. The glaciated northeast slopes provide an impressive foreground for the expanse of Waldo Lake.

Waldo Lake from Fuji Mountain.

FUJI MOUNTAIN

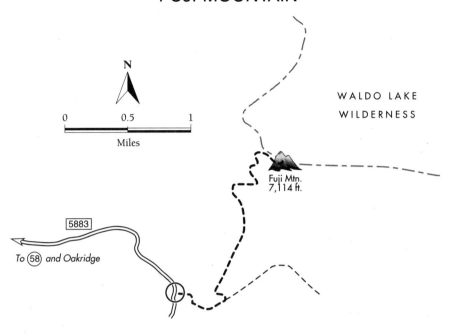

N

0   0.5   1

Miles

WALDO LAKE
WILDERNESS

Fuji Mtn.
7,114 ft.

5883

To 58 and Oakridge

---

58 RIGDON LAKES LOOP

General description:	A day hike or overnight backpack trip along the shores of Waldo Lake to Rigdon Lakes in the Waldo Lake Wilderness.
Location:	About 35 miles east of Oakridge.
Maps:	Waldo Mountain USGS; Waldo Lake Wilderness and Recreation Area, Willamette National Forest.
Length:	9.6-mile loop.
Elevation:	5,420 to 5,600 feet.
Best season:	Summer and fall.
Permit:	Permit required for day and overnight hikes; self issue at trailhead.
For more information:	Oakridge Ranger District, Willamette National Forest.

Key points:
    0.0 Trailhead.
    0.5 Rejoin the Waldo Lake Trail, go left.
    2.7 Rigdon Lakes Trail; stay left.
    3.9 Turn right onto the Wahanna Lake Trail.
    5.4 Go right onto the Rigdon Lakes Trail.
    7.4 Rejoin the Waldo Lake Trail; turn left.
    9.6 Trailhead.

RIGDON LAKES LOOP

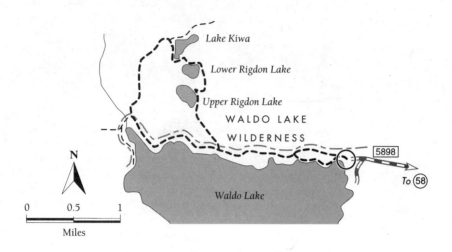

Finding the trailhead: From Oakridge, drive about 23 miles east on Oregon Highway 58, then turn left (north) on the paved Waldo Lake Road (Forest Road 5897). Continue about 12 miles to North Waldo Campground, then park in the boat parking area just north (right) of the boat ramp. The Waldo Lake Trail is next to the picnic area on the north side of the parking lot and is marked.

The hike: A large area north of Waldo Lake burned in summer 1996. There is likely to be an unusual amount of deadfall along this hike, as well as hazards such as standing dead trees. The Rigdon Lakes area is heavily used and some areas are closed to camping for rehabilitation. Please avoid these closed areas.

The trail wanders away from the picnic area toward the lakeshore and almost immediately comes to a trail on the right, marked Taylor Burn Road. Remember this junction for the return. For now, continue straight ahead. Another trail merges from the left; this is the trail to the boat launch area. In a few more yards, you'll meet the marked turnoff for the Lake Shore Trail. Turn left here to make a slight detour along the edge of Waldo Lake. The Lake Shore Trail rejoins the Waldo Lake Trail in about 0.5 mile, making a sharp left turn. Now the trail wanders away from the lake into the thick forest, passing several small ponds. After 2.2 miles, you'll pass the junction with the Rigdon Lakes Trail; this will be your return. Go left, staying on the Waldo Lake Trail for another 1.2 miles. In this section, the trail skirts the lakeshore in several places. At Dam Camp, turn right onto the Wahanna Lake Trail. But first, check out the outlet stream for Waldo Lake, which is the head of the Middle Fork of the Willamette River. It's just a few yards up the Waldo Lake Trail from the junction.

Turning away from Waldo Lake, the Wahanna Lake Trail skirts the edge of the Middle Fork canyon, and there are sometimes hints of it through the heavy forest. After 1.5 miles, turn right (east) onto the Rigdon Lakes Trail. The first lake is actually Lake Kiwa, which you come upon almost immediately. Next, the trail passes the two Rigdon Lakes, then heads south for the Waldo Lake Trail, which it reaches 2 miles from the Wahanna Trail. Turn left to return to the trailhead in 2.2 miles.

59 WALDO LAKE SHORELINE TRAIL

General description:	A day hike along the edge of Waldo Lake with views of the Three Sisters.
Location:	About 32 miles east of Oakridge.
Maps:	Waldo Lake USGS; Waldo Lake Wilderness and Recreation Area, Willamette National Forest.
Difficulty:	Easy.
Length:	4.2 miles round-trip.
Elevation:	5,420 to 5,420 feet.
Best season:	Summer and fall.
Permit:	Permit required for day and overnight hikes; self issue at trailhead.
For more information:	Oakridge Ranger District, Willamette National Forest.

Key points:
    0.0   Trailhead.
    0.5   Waldo Lake Trail joins from left.
    1.7   South Waldo Shelter.
    2.1   Three Sisters viewpoint.

Finding the trailhead: From Oakridge, drive about 23 miles east on Oregon Highway 58, then turn left (north) on the paved Waldo Lake Road (Forest Road 5897). Continue 6.4 miles, then turn left on the marked, paved road to Shadow Bay Campground. Go past the campground and park in the boat parking area. The marked Shoreline Trail is on the north side of the parking lot.

The hike: Follow the trail along the edge of the lake as it swings around Shadow Bay. About 0.5 mile from the trailhead, the Waldo Lake Trail joins from the left. Although the trail is not at the water's edge, there are a number of opportunities to get to the edge of the lake, and it is usually visible through the trees. You reach South Waldo Shelter, an Adirondack-style cabin, about 1.7 miles from the trailhead. The main trail goes left of the cabin and is joined by the South Waldo Trail from the left. Stay right across several footbridges

Waldo Lake.

as the trail passes near some open meadows. About 0.4 mile from the cabin, the trail reaches the lake again at its southwest corner. After this point the trail turns north along the west shore of the lake and continues about 10 miles to North Waldo Campground. Your hike ends here, where the trail moves inland. Walk to the water's edge for a view of this majestic lake with the Three Sisters rising above the treeline to the north.

WALDO LAKE SHORELINE TRAIL
BETTY LAKE

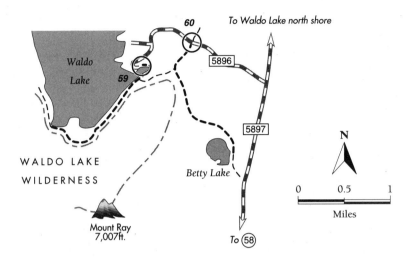

60 *BETTY LAKE*

General description: A day hike past a series of small lakes to Betty Lake.

Location: About 28 miles east of Oakridge.

Maps: Waldo Lake USGS; Waldo Lake Wilderness and Recreation Area, Willamette National Forest.

Difficulty: Easy.

Length: 3.4 miles round-trip.

Elevation: 5,500 to 5,700 feet.

Best season: Summer and fall.

Permit: None.

For more information: Oakridge Ranger District, Willamette National Forest.

Key points:
- 0.0 Trailhead.
- 0.5 Turn left onto the Betty Lake Trail.
- 1.7 Betty Lake.

Finding the trailhead: From Oakridge, drive about 20.7 miles southeast on Oregon Highway 58, then turn left (north) on the paved road to Waldo Lake (Forest Road 5897). Continue about 6.4 miles, then turn left on the paved Shadow Bay road. The trailhead is 1 mile farther, and is marked for the Waldo Lake Trail. There is limited parking on the left.

Walking the Betty Lake Trail.

The hike: Take the Waldo Lake Trail left (south), which is marked Shadow Bay. Follow this trail about 0.5 mile through noble fir forest, then turn left at the marked junction with the Betty Lake Trail. It climbs steeply for a short distance, then levels out as the trail passes three small, shallow lakes. Betty Lake is about 1.2 miles from the junction. This is a beautiful lake and seems less visited than some of the other lakes in the area. For those who wish to do a short backpack trip (perhaps with small children), there are excellent campsites along the southeast shore of the lake. The trail continues about 0.5 mile to the Waldo Lake Road, but you will have to return the way you came unless you have done a car shuttle.

ADDITIONAL TRAILS

Fisher Creek Trail starts from Forest Road 750 and climbs out of Fisher Creek to Forest Road 254.

Winchester Ridge Trail starts from FR 254 and traverses a long ridge above the Eddeeleo Lakes, joining the Waldo Mountain Trail.

Waldo Mountain Trail starts from Forest Road 2424 and climbs Waldo Mountain. It continues east to join the Salmon Lakes Trail.

Salmon Lakes Trail also starts from FR 2424 and goes to Lower and Upper Salmon Lakes.

Divide Trail begins at the end of Forest Road 381 and ends at the south end of Waldo Lake at the Waldo Lake Trail.

Wehanna Trail continues north from Lake Kiwa, ending at the Taylor Burn Trailhead.

Whig and Torrey Trail leaves Forest Road 514 and passes Whig and Torrey lakes, then rejoins FR 514.

Waldo Lake Trail circles Waldo Lake, with trailheads at the North Waldo Campground and Shadow Bay Campground, accessible from Forest Road 5897.

Pacific Crest National Scenic Trail (PCST) starts at the Irish Lake trailhead, passes Charlton Butte, The Twins, and Maiden Peak, then continues south to Willamette Pass on Oregon Highway 58.

The Twins Trail starts at Charlton Lake, on Forest Road 5897 east of Waldo Lake, climbs over The Twins, and ends at FR 5897.

Charlton Lake Trail starts from Forest Road 5898 east of Waldo Lake and ends at Charlton Lake on the PCST.

Bobby Lake Trail starts from FR 5897 opposite the Betty Lake Trail and goes east to the PCST and Bobby Lake.

Gold Lake Trail starts from Gold Lake on Forest Road 500 and parallels FR 5897 to meet the Bobby Lake Trail.

Maiden Lake Trail leaves the PCST north of Rosary Lakes and traverses the south slopes of Maiden Peak to Maiden Lake, then turns north, providing an alternate route to the top of Maiden Peak.

Lower Fuji Mountain Trail starts from FR 5897 north of Willamette Pass, crosses the South Waldo Trail, and climbs to meet the upper Fuji Mountain Trail.

South Waldo Trail starts from FR 5898 west of Willamette Pass, and ends at Waldo Lake's south end. It crosses the lower Fuji Mountain Trail, and a side trail goes down Ray Creek to FR 5897.

Deception Butte Trail starts from OR 58 just west of Oakridge and climbs Deception Butte.

Tire Mountain Trail starts from Forest Road 1911 north of Oakridge, climbs Tire Mountain, then continues west to Forest Road 5824.

Larison Creek Trail starts from Forest Road 21, south of Oakridge, and follows Larison Creek to the west, ending at Forest Road 101.

DIAMOND PEAK

OVERVIEW

The 52,737-acre Diamond Peak Wilderness surrounds 8,744-foot Diamond Peak, the centerpiece of the region. A glacier-carved volcano, the mountain has four distinct summits. The Pacific Crest National Scenic Trail runs north to south through the Wilderness and passes along the east slopes of Diamond Peak. The peak was named for John Diamond, who, with others, first climbed it in 1852 while exploring the area for a possible wagon road. The wagon road became known was the Free Emigrant Road, and it was in use over Emigrant Pass by 1853. Use picked up by 1870 when the route was upgraded into the Oregon Central Military Wagon Road. Several of the following hikes use this historic road as an access route. Numerous small lakes dot the heavily timbered Wilderness. Three large lakes, Summit Lake, Crescent Lake, and Odell Lake, border the wilderness area.

61 DIAMOND FALLS

General description:	A day hike to three spectacular waterfalls.
Location:	About 19 miles east of Oakridge.
Maps:	Diamond Peak USGS; Diamond Peak Wilderness Imus Geographics; Willamette National Forest.
Difficulty:	Easy.
Length:	3.2-mile loop.
Elevation:	4,000 to 4,300 feet.
Best season:	Summer and fall.
Permit:	None.
For more information:	Oakridge Ranger District, Willamette National Forest.

DIAMOND FALLS

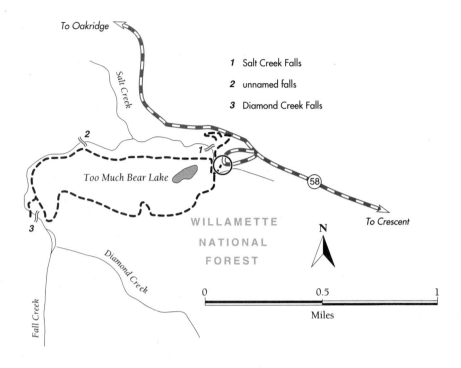

To Oakridge

Salt Creek

1 Salt Creek Falls
2 unnamed falls
3 Diamond Creek Falls

2

Too Much Bear Lake

1

58

To Crescent

3

WILLAMETTE

NATIONAL

FOREST

N

Diamond Creek

Fall Creek

0   0.5   1
Miles

Key points:
- 0.0   Trailhead at Salt Creek Falls parking lot.
- 0.3   Lower Salt Creek Falls viewpoint.
- 0.6   Diamond Creek Falls Trail.
- 0.7   Loop junction, turn right.
- 1.8   Diamond Creek Falls spur trail.
- 3.1   Loop junction, turn right.
- 3.2   Salt Creek Falls parking lot.

Finding the trailhead: From Oakridge, drive about 18.8 miles south-east on Oregon Highway 58, then turn right (south) at the sign for Salt Creek Falls. Follow the paved road to the parking area and information display.

The hike: Put up with the throngs of tourists gawking at Salt Creek Falls and do some gawking yourself. It's a very impressive waterfall. Then continue north along the paved path and walk 0.3 mile down to the lower viewpoint. Here you get a clear view of the entire length of the falls. Salt Creek Falls are a result of glacial action. The main glacier in Salt Creek deepened that canyon at a greater rate than the tributaries. When the ice melted, it left the side valleys perched high above the floor of Salt Creek.

Salt Creek Falls.

The tributary streams pour out of the hanging valleys, forming several waterfalls in this area.

Return to the upper viewpoint, then follow the paved trail south to the marked start of the Diamond Falls Trail. Cross the bridge across Salt Creek, then follow the trail a hundred yards or so to a T junction. Turn left (north) here, toward Too Much Bear Lake. The lake itself appears shortly to the left of the trail. It's disappointingly small and shallow for a lake with such an interesting name. The trail closely follows the rim of Salt Creek canyon westward. Watch for smooth sections of basalt, planed off by the ancient glaciers. In a few places you can see glacial polish, where the moving ice buffed the rock. Cooling basalt flows sometimes form vertical columns, as it contracts and minute cracks form. Here you can see the fractures, which make the rock outcrops look as though they were built by hand from irregular stone tiles.

A marked viewpoint gives a distant glimpse of a waterfall on Fall Creek, then the trail swings southwest and south and follows the creek upstream. An unmarked spur trail goes right (west), descends to the creek, and follows it upstream a few yards to Diamond Falls, which seem to be misnamed because they're really on Fall Creek. The falls cascade down a 60-degree slab of rock. Return to the main trail, which passes a viewpoint overlooking the fall from above, then reaches a junction with the Vivian Lake Trail. Don't be startled if you hear the sudden roar of a freight train; the main tracks of the Southern Pacific Railroad are out of sight in the forest just above the falls. Turn left, staying with the Diamond Falls Trail. It crosses a road, then contours east around a point, crosses a second road, then descends to meet the loop junction. Turn right (east) and return to the Salt Creek Falls parking area.

62 *VIVIAN LAKE*

General description:	A day hike or overnight backpack to an alpine lake in the Diamond Peak Wilderness.
Location:	About 20 miles southeast of Oakridge.
Maps:	Diamond Peak USGS; Diamond Peak Wilderness Imus Geographics; Willamette National Forest.
Difficulty:	Moderate.
Length:	6.8 miles round-trip.
Elevation:	5,320 to 6,000 feet.
Best season:	Summer.
Permit:	Permit required for day and overnight hikes; self issue at trailhead.
For more information:	Oakridge Ranger District, Willamette National Forest.

Key points:
- 0.0 Trailhead.
- 1.0 Junction with Mount Yoran Trail; continue straight.
- 1.3 Spur trail goes left; turn right (east).
- 2.0 Pass.
- 3.4 Vivian Lake.

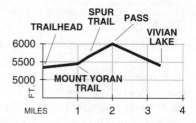

Finding the trailhead: From Oakridge at the post office turnoff, drive east 2 miles on Oregon Highway 58, then turn right (south) on Forest Road 23, the Hills Creek Reservoir Road. The first 15 miles are paved, then FR 23 becomes gravel. About 18.2 miles from OR 58, turn left (north) at the Vivian Lake trailhead.

The hike: The Vivian Lake Trail leaves the trailhead clearcut behind in a few dozen yards, then climbs gently through a mountain hemlock, Douglas-fir, and subalpine fir forest. Rocky and picturesque Notch Lake appears on the left. Then, 1 mile from the trailhead, the turnoff to Mount Yoran is encountered. Go straight, remaining on the Vivian Lake Trail. The trail climbs a bit more now, but the serious climbing begins after passing a marked spur trail. Still, the trail is only steep in spots as it works its way to the crest of a 6,000-foot ridge, crossing a broad pass. It drops rapidly on the east side of the ridge, passes a couple of small lakes, then swings north past a meadow. The spur trail to Vivian Lake is marked and goes west a hundred yards or so to reach the east end of the lake. Walk around the lake to its northwest shore for a view of Mount Yoran reflected in the green waters.

Vivian Lake.

VIVIAN LAKE • DIVIDE LAKE
HEMLOCK BUTTE

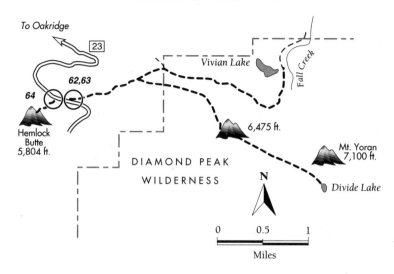

63 *DIVIDE LAKE*

General description:	A day hike or overnight backpack to an apine lake nestled below the steep slopes of Mount Yoran in the Diamond Peak Wilderness. This hike offers excellent views.
Location:	About 20 miles southeast of Oakridge.
Maps:	Diamond Peak USGS; Diamond Peak Wilderness Imus Geographics; Willamette National Forest.
Difficulty:	Moderate.
Length:	7.8 miles round-trip.
Elevation:	5,320 to 6,480 feet.
Best season:	Summer and fall.
Permit:	Permit required for day and overnight hikes; self issue at trailhead.
For more information:	Oakridge Ranger District, Willamette National Forest.

Key points:
- 0.0 Trailhead.
- 1.0 Mount Yoran Trail; turn right.
- 3.9 Divide Lake.

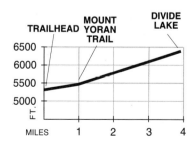

Finding the trailhead: From Oakridge at the post office turnoff, drive east 2 miles on Oregon Highway 58, then turn right (south) on Forest Road 23, the Hills Creek Reservoir Road. The first 15 miles are paved, then FR 23 becomes gravel. About 18.2 miles from OR 58, turn left (north) at the Vivian Lake trailhead.

The hike: The hike starts on the Vivian Lake Trail; just past rocky Notch Lake, turn right (east) onto the Mount Yoran Trail at a marked junction. The trail climbs steadily through the parklike fir and mountain hemlock forest, gradually turning to the southeast as the slope steepens. The trail climbs onto the long northwest ridge of Mount Yoran and follows the ridge toward the peak, sometimes visible through the trees ahead. At a saddle, there's a fairly good view toward the north, with Broken Top and South Sister visible in the distance. Part of the Vivian Lake basin, including the meadow near the lake, can be seen from a closer viewpoint. As the trail continues along the ridge, dipping in and out of saddles and climbing over small knobs, there are occasional glimpses of Diamond Peak to the south.

About 0.5 mile from Divide Lake, there's a great view of the rocky spire of Mount Yoran. The trail crosses at the foot of a talus slope below the peak, then descends slightly to reach Divide Lake. There are a few campsites to the west of the lake, for those backpacking. The lake is not deep, but the rugged setting makes it a jewel nonetheless.

---

64   HEMLOCK BUTTE

General description:	A day hike to a rocky butte overlooking Mount Yoran and Diamond Peak.
Location:	About 20 miles southeast of Oakridge.
Maps:	Diamond Peak USGS; Willamette National Forest.
Difficulty:	Easy.
Length:	1 mile round-trip.
Elevation:	5,330 to 5,804 feet.
Best season:	Summer and fall.
Permit:	None.
For more information:	Oakridge Ranger District, Willamette National Forest.

See Map on Page 171

Key points:
0.0   Trailhead.
0.5   Hemlock Butte.

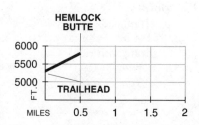

Finding the trailhead: From Oakridge at the post office turnoff, drive east 2 miles on Oregon Highway 58, then turn right (south) on Forest Road 23, the Hills Creek Reservoir Road. The first 15 miles are paved, then FR 23 becomes gravel. About 18.1 miles from OR 58, park at the Hemlock Butte trailhead on the right (south) side of the road.

The hike: This short but rewarding hike starts at the hiker sign on the right (south) side of the road about 0.1 mile west of the Vivian Lake trailhead. The trail climbs steadily through a mountain hemlock forest (of course!), with subalpine and grand fir present as well. Switchbacks lead up the northeast ridge and to the base of the summit block. The trail appears to end, but a last switchback to the right leads to a short, well-trodden scramble to the summit. The inevitable signs of the former fire lookout structure are here in the form of melted bits of glass and a few foundation bolts. The view is open in all directions, with an especially fine view of the Swift Creek and Bear Creek drainages on the northwest slopes of Diamond Peak.

Diamond Peak.

65 MAIDEN PEAK

General description:	A long day hike to 7,800-foot Maiden Peak, which offers fines views of the central Cascades.
Location:	About 27 miles southeast of Oakridge.
Maps:	Waldo Lake, The Twins USGS; Diamond Peak Wilderness Imus Geographic; Willamette National Forest.
Difficulty:	Difficult.
Length:	11 miles round-trip.
Elevation:	4,940 to 7,818 feet.
Best season:	Summer and fall.
Permit:	None.
For more information:	Oakridge Ranger District, Willamette National Forest.

Key points:

- 0.0 Trailhead.
- 1.7 Skyline Creek.
- 2.7 Cross the Pacific Crest National Scenic Trail.
- 5.0 Maiden Peak.

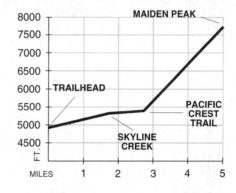

The Three Sisters from Maiden Peak.

MAIDEN PEAK

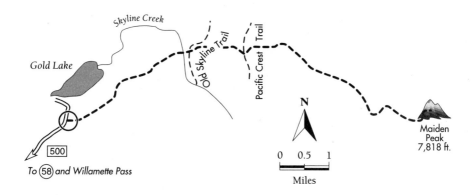

Finding the trailhead: From Oakridge, drive about 21 miles east on Oregon Highway 58, then turn left (north) on the Gold Lake gravel road (Forest Road 500). Go about 2 miles and park at the trailhead for Maiden Peak.

The hike: The trail climbs away from the road, then switches back to the northeast. It continues across the densely forested slope, climbing gradually about 1.7 miles to Skyline Creek. This spot, also known as Wait Here Camp, is the last place to get water on the ascent. An abandoned segment of the Pacific Crest National Scenic Trail (PCST) crosses here, following the creek. The PCST is shown in its old location on the USGS maps, but is updated on the Imus Geographic map.

Continue about 1 mile, climbing more steeply now, to the current (and marked) PCST, which crosses your trail at right angles. Continue on the Maiden Peak Trail as it continues to climb steeply for about 0.3 mile before the ascent moderates. The next mile is a gradual climb through more open forest and there are occasional hints of the great view to come. Watch for pieces of solid steel wire lying on the ground next to the trail. This was the old single wire phone line to the summit fire lookout. Originally it would have been strung on donut-shaped insulators wired to the trees, but these have all been removed. As the slope steepens for the final climb, the trail swings right, then left in a broad switchback. At the end of the switchback, you are about 0.5 mile from the summit and 600 feet below it. The mountain hemlock trees are shorter and stockier now because of the harsher climate near the top of the mountain. Finally, whitebark pine and subalpine fir replace the hemlock. An unmarked trail comes in from the right here, climbing directly up the slope. Note this intersection carefully for the descent to avoid taking the wrong trail.

The actual summit is marked by a pile of rocks, probably the remains of the old lookout cabin. Pieces of cast iron stove and melted glass are scattered around. The lookout person had a superb view in all directions. Much of the area covered by this guidebook can be seen. Mount Thielsen is visible to the south. Southwest lie Odell and Crescent lakes, and above Odell Lake are Lakeview and Diamond Peaks. To the west some of the ski runs at Willamette Pass Ski Area are visible. The small lake to the left and below the ski runs is Rosary Lake. To the northwest is Mount Ray and Waldo Lake. Visible far to the north are the Three Sisters and Mount Jefferson.

66 *ROSARY LAKES*

General description:	A day hike on the Pacific Crest National Scenic Trail to Rosary Lakes.
Location:	About 26 miles southeast of Oakridge.
Maps:	Willamette Pass, Odell Lake USGS; Diamond Peak Wilderness Imus Geographics; Deschutes National Forest.
Difficulty:	Moderate.
Length:	6 miles round-trip.
Elevation:	5,100 to 5,707 feet.
Best season:	Summer and fall.
Permit:	None.
For more information:	Crescent Ranger District, Deschutes National Forest.

Key points:

0.0   Trailhead; go right on the PCST.

3.0   Lower Rosary Lake.

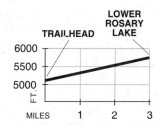

Finding the trailhead: From Oakridge, drive about 26 miles east on Oregon Highway 58, then turn left at the marked Pacific Crest National Scenic Trail (PCST) trailhead, which is just past Willamette Pass.

The hike: Follow the Pacific Crest National Scenic Trail as it traverses the slopes eastbound, above Odell Lake. There is a junction a few yards from the trailhead; turn right and follow the PCST as it climbs east along the slope above Odell Lake. There are occasional glimpses of the lake through the forest. The tall, stately trees are mostly Douglas-fir and noble fir. After about 2.5 miles, the trail veers left and enters the drainage of Rosary Creek. The stream is too far away to hear, though. A talus slope on the left marks a point just before Lower Rosary Lake, which appears in another hundred yards. This heart-shaped lake is much larger than the other two Rosary Lakes. It forms a perfect mirror for Pulpit Rock, 600 feet above the lake.

ROSARY LAKES
EAGLE ROCK

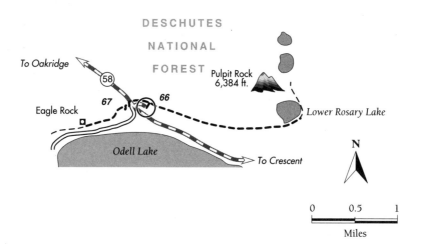

DESCHUTES

NATIONAL

To Oakridge

FOREST

Pulpit Rock
6,384 ft.

Eagle Rock

Lower Rosary Lake

Odell Lake

To Crescent

N

0   0.5   1

Miles

67   *EAGLE ROCK*

General description:	A day hike along the Pacific Crest National Scenic Trail to a rock overlooking Odell Lake.
Location:	About 26 miles southeast of Oakridge.
Maps:	Willamette Pass USGS; Diamond Peak Wilderness Imus Geographics; Deschutes National Forest.
Difficulty:	Easy.
Length:	1.4 miles round-trip.
Elevation:	5,100 to 5,200 feet.
Best season:	Summer and fall.
Permit:	None.
For more information:	Crescent Ranger District, Deschutes National Forest.

Key points:
   0.0 Trailhead.
   0.7 Eagle Rock.

Finding the trailhead: From Oakridge, drive about 26 miles east on Oregon Highway 58, then turn left at the Pacific Crest National Scenic Trail (PCST) trailhead just past Willamette Pass.

The hike: At the junction a few yards from the trailhead, turn left and walk the PCST around the cinder storage building, then cross the highway. The trail is well marked on both sides of the highway. The roar of the road

Odell Lake from Eagle Rock.

is soon left behind as the trail climbs the beautiful forested slopes. After about 0.2 mile the trail comes out onto the slope west of Odell Lake; there are a few glimpses of the lake. The trail is nearly level in this section. Eagle Rock is an outcrop on the left side of the trail with sweeping views of Odell Lake and the Diamond Peak Wilderness. The prominent triangular peak above the lake is Lakeview Peak.

68 HIDDEN LAKE

General description:	A day hike or easy overnight backpack on the Pacific Crest National Scenic Trail to a series of alpine lakes in the Diamond Peak Wilderness.
Location:	About 26 miles southeast of Oakridge.
Maps:	Willamette Pass USGS; Diamond Peak Wilderness Imus Geographics; Deschutes National Forest.
Difficulty:	Moderate.
Length:	11.2 miles round-trip.
Elevation:	5,100 to 5,350 feet.
Best season:	Summer and fall.
Permit:	None.
For more information:	Crescent Ranger District, Deschutes National Forest.

See Map on Page 180

Key points:

0.0	Trailhead.
1.5	Pengra Pass
3.0	Midnight Lake.
5.6	Hidden Lake.

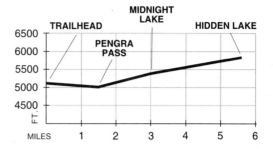

Finding the trailhead: From Oakridge, drive about 26 miles east on Oregon Highway 58, then turn left at the Pacific Crest National Scenic Trail (PCST) trailhead just past Willamette Pass.

The hike: Walk up the trail a few yards to a junction, then turn left on the Pacific Crest National Scenic Trail, marked for Summit Lake. The trail passes behind the cinder storage building, then crosses the highway. It is marked on both sides of the highway. The trail climbs gently up the hillside, then contours around to Pengra Pass, about 1.5 miles from the highway. Here it crosses a dirt road then starts to climb again, passing through a noble fir forest. About 1.5 miles from Pengra Pass, the trail passes a short spur trail to Midnight Lake, which is well worth the side trip. The next lake is on the right and forms a near perfect arrowhead shape, hence the name Arrowhead Lake. From here, it is about 1 mile to the end of the hike at Hidden Lake, which is barely visible through the trees from the main trail.

Pengra Pass is named for Byron J. Pengra, who explored the area and discovered the pass. Pengra was instrumental in surveying the route of the Central Oregon Military Wagon Road, which was completed in 1867. The wagon road crossed the Cascades at Emigrant Pass and rapidly became a vital link between the western Oregon settlements and Boise, Idaho.

69 *YORAN LAKE*

General description:	A day hike to Yoran Lake in the Diamond Peak Wilderness.
Location:	About 29 miles southeast of Oakridge.
Maps:	Willamette Pass USGS; Diamond Peak Wilderness Imus Geographics; Deschutes National Forest.
Difficulty:	Moderate.
Length:	8 miles round-trip or 10.5-mile optional loop.
Elevation:	4,800 to 5,950 feet.
Best season:	Summer and fall.
Permit:	Permit required for day and overnight hikes; self issue at trailhead.
For more information:	Crescent Ranger District, Deschutes National Forest.

HIDDEN LAKE
YORAN LAKE

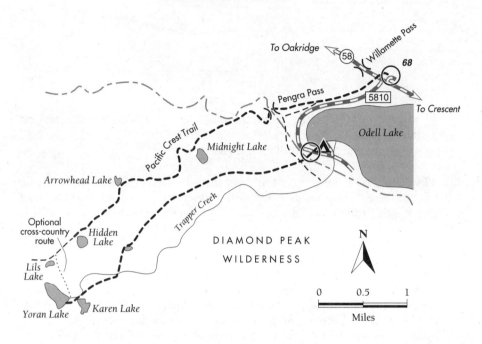

Key points:

0.0 Trailhead.
0.1 Go straight on the Yoran Lake Trail.
3.0 Pass a shallow, unnamed lake.
4.0 Yoran Lake.

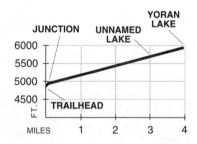

Finding the trailhead: From Oakridge, drive about 27 miles east on Oregon Highway 58, crossing Willamette Pass, then turn right on the paved road marked "Odell Lake West Access." The Yoran Lake trailhead is on the right after about 2 miles, just before the Trapper Creek Campground sign.

The hike: Follow the trail across the railroad tracks. Use caution—the eastbound trains come out of a tunnel less than 1 mile away and appear with little warning. A trail junction is met about 0.1 mile after the tracks. Continue straight ahead on the marked Yoran Lake Trail. The trail climbs steadily but gradually through continuous forest. Here, the Cascade forest is dominated by noble fir, with more mountain hemlock appearing as you climb.

Diamond Peak above Yoran Lake.

The trail passes a small, shallow lake, which is to the left (south); this signals the 3-mile point. After about 0.8 mile, you'll get a glimpse of Karen Lake, also to the left of the trail. A slight descent leads to Yoran Lake and the trail's end. There is a good view of Diamond Peak, but Yoran Peak is hidden.

For those with map and compass skills, it's possible to make an interesting loop trip with the Hidden Lake hike. The connecting link is about 0.7 mile of easy cross-country hiking from Yoran Lake to Lils Lake. To do this, proceed northwest along the east shore of the lake. From the north end of the lake, turn more to the north and you'll run into tiny Lils Lake, nestled below the unmistakable Pacific Crest National Scenic Trail (PCST). Turn right and walk about 0.5 mile to Hidden Lake (see Hike 68 for details). When you reach Pengra Pass on the return, instead of going to the PCST on OR 58, turn right and follow an old road to the south. Just before reaching the railroad tracks, take a trail to the right that parallels the tracks and leads to the junction at the beginning of the Yoran Lake Trail. Turn left and walk a few yards to the trailhead. This cutoff is 0.8 mile long, and the total loop distance is 10.5 miles.

General description:	A day hike or an easy overnight backpack to a tranquil alpine lake with a rugged backdrop in the Diamond Peak Wilderness.
Location:	About 35 miles southeast of Oakridge.
Maps:	Willamette Pass, Odell Lake, Crescent Lake USGS; Diamond Peak Wilderness Imus Geographics; Deschutes National Forest.
Difficulty:	Moderate.
Length:	5.4 miles round-trip.
Elevation:	4,800 to 5,630 feet.
Best season:	Summer and fall.
Permit:	None.
For more information:	Crescent Ranger District, Deschutes National Forest.

Key points:
  0.0   Trailhead.
  2.7   Fawn Lake.

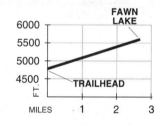

Fawn Lake.

FAWN LAKE

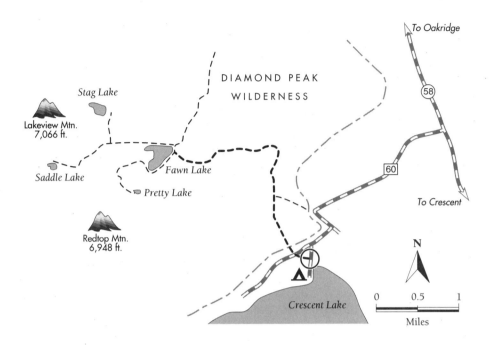

Finding the trailhead: From Oakridge, drive about 33 miles east on Oregon Highway 58, then turn right (south) at the sign for Crescent Lake Campground. Go about 2.2 miles, then, just before the campground entrance, turn right into the trailhead parking lot. The trail starts from the north side of the parking lot.

The hike: The marked Fawn Lake Trail starts by crossing the paved Forest Road 60, then continues across a trail that parallels the road. The wilderness boundary is passed almost immediately. For the first 1 mile or so, the trail is nearly level and passes through an open lodgepole pine forest. After crossing an old road, the trail begins to climb through a Douglas-fir forest. You'll also see, mixed with the firs, a few ponderosa pines and mountain hemlock. After about 2 miles, the trail turns west and climbs at an easier rate. The forest also opens up and becomes dominated by lodgepole pine again. After a few zigzags to head minor gullies, the trail reaches Fawn Lake. This shallow lake is about a 0.5 mile across and serves as a reflector for Lakeview Mountain to the west, and Redtop Mountain to the southwest.

Several trails branch out from Fawn Lake and make it possible to explore some of the other lakes in this scenic area.

General description:	A day hike along the shores of Summit Lake with excellent views of Diamond Peak in the Oregon Cascades Recreation Area.
Location:	About 45 miles southeast of Oakridge.
Maps:	Cowhorn Mountain USGS; Diamond Peak Wilderness Imus Geographics; Deschutes National Forest.
Difficulty:	Easy.
Length:	1.2 miles round-trip.
Elevation:	5,560 feet.
Best season:	Summer and fall.
Permit:	None.
For more information:	Crescent Ranger District, Deschutes National Forest.

Key points:
0.0   Trailhead.
0.2   Summit Creek.
0.6   Summit Lake view.

Finding the trailhead: From Oakridge, drive about 33.4 miles southeast on Oregon Highway 58, past Odell Lake. Turn right (west) on Forest

Summit Lake.

SUMMIT LAKE
PACIFIC CREST NATIONAL
SCENIC TRAIL (SUMMIT LAKE)

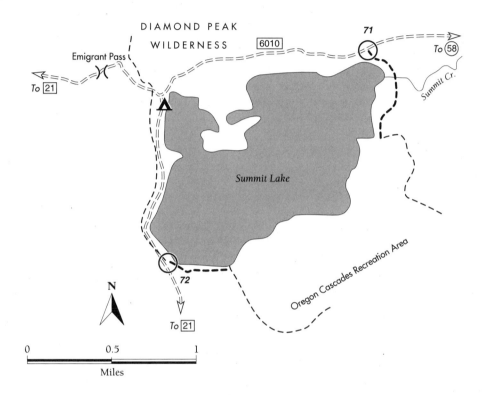

Road 60. Continue 6.2 miles along Crescent Lake to Forest Road 6010. Turn right (northwest) on this dirt road. A high-clearance vehicle is recommended, but a standard car can drive this road with care. Continue 5 miles to the trailhead on the left. Summit Lake is visible from the trailhead.

The hike: The trail initially follows the shore of Summit Lake to the left (southeast). After about 0.2 mile, it wanders farther from the lake and crosses Summit Creek on a footbridge. After a pleasant and nearly level ramble through open lodgepole pine forest, Summit Lake becomes visible again on the right. Leave the trail, walk to the lakeshore, then work your way south for about 150 yards until Diamond Peak becomes visible to the north. Summit Lake is about 1.5 miles by 1 mile, and is well named because it lies virtually on the crest of the Cascade Range.

72 PACIFIC CREST NATIONAL SCENIC TRAIL (SUMMIT LAKE)

General description:	An easy day hike along the shores of beautiful Summit Lake in the Oregon Cascades Recreation Area.
Location:	About 47 miles southeast of Oakridge.
Maps:	Emigrant Butte USGS; Diamond Peak Wilderness Imus Geographics; Deschutes National Forest.
Difficulty:	Easy.
Length:	1 miles round-trip.
Elevation:	5,560 feet.
Best season:	Summer and fall.
Permit:	None.
For more information:	Crescent Ranger District, Deschutes National Forest.

See Map on Page 185

Key points:
- 0.0 Trailhead.
- 0.5 Diamond Peak view.

Finding the trailhead: From Oakridge, drive about 33.4 miles southeast on Oregon Highway 58, past Odell Lake. Turn right (west) on Forest Road 60. Continue 6.2 miles along Crescent Lake to Forest Road 6010. Turn right (northwest) on this dirt road. A high-clearance vehicle is recommended, but a standard car can drive this road with care. Continue 6.4 miles, then turn left on FR 6010 at the northwest corner of Summit Lake. Continue about 1.2 miles to the point where the road starts to leave the lakeshore. The marked Pacific Crest National Scenic Trail (PCST) crosses the road here. Park in the wide place along the road; there is no specific trailhead.

The hike: Follow the Pacific Crest National Scenic Trail to the southeast as it follows the lake's edge. After about 0.5 mile of easy walking through the lodgepole pine forest, the trail leaves the lake. A short walk north brings you to the lake, with expansive views of the Diamond Peak Wilderness to the north.

Of course, the PCST can be used for a longer hike—all the way to Mexico if desired!

ADDITIONAL TRAILS

Vivian Lake Trail continues from Diamond Creek Falls up Fall Creek, past Fall Creek Falls, and then to Vivian Lake.

Trail 3699 is a long trail that traverses the western side of the Diamond Peak Wilderness from Forest Road 23 at Swift Creek to Forest Road 380 near Emigrant Pass. Several side trails lead west to Happy Lake, Blue Lake, and Corrigan Lake, and out to trailheads.

Diamond Rockpile Trail starts from Forest Road 2160 goes past Diamond

Rockpile and Rockpile Lake to join the PCST south of Diamond Peak.

Pacific Crest National Scenic Trail continues south from Hidden Lake along the east slopes of Diamond Peak to FR 380 at Emigrant Pass. After passing Summit Lake, it continues past Cowhorn Mountain to a trailhead at Windigo Pass on Forest Road 90.

Diamond View Lake Trail starts near Trapper Creek Campground on Odell Lake, passes Diamond View Lake, and ends at the west end of Crescent Lake on Forest Road 60.

Snell Lake Trail starts from FR 6010 and goes past Snell Lake. One branch goes east to the Diamond View Lake Trail and the other west to the PCST.

Meek Lake Trail also starts from FR 6010, passes Meek Lake, meanders south to meet the Summit Lake Trail, and continues into the Windy Lakes area.

Indigo Lake Trail starts from Forest Road 2154 southwest of Oakridge and goes to Indigo Lake.

MOUNT THIELSEN WILDERNESS

OVERVIEW

The Mount Thielsen Wilderness covers 55,100 acres straddling the southern Oregon Cascades. The Wilderness features alpine parks and lakes as well as extensive forest. The centerpiece of the Wilderness, Mount Thielsen, rises to 9,178 feet. Its spirelike summit is unusual for a High Cascade volcano. It is a Matterhorn-style peak, like Mount Washington and Three Fingered Jack to the north. The fact that Mount Thielsen has been eroded so heavily by glaciers, without any new volcanic material being added, shows that the mountain ceased erupting before the last two or three major ice ages. Its slender summit spire is struck by lightning so often that it is nicknamed the "lightning rod of the Cascades."

73 *MILLER LAKE LOOP*

General description:	An easy, level day hike around Miller Lake on the edge of the Mount Thielsen Wilderness.
Location:	12 miles west of Chumult.
Maps:	Miller Lake USGS; Rogue–Umpqua Divide, Boulder Creek, and Mount Thielsen wilderness areas in Winema National Forest.
Difficulty:	Easy.
Length:	4.7-mile loop.
Elevation:	5,640 feet.
Best season:	Summer and fall.
Permit:	None.
For more information:	Chemult Ranger District, Winema National Forest.

MILLER LAKE LOOP
MAIDU LAKE

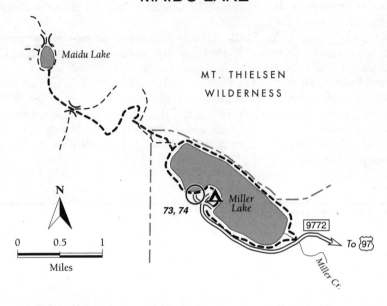

Key points:
- 0.0 Trailhead.
- 1.8 Road; go left on the Maidu Lake Trail.
- 4.0 Miller Lake Trail; turn left.
- 4.7 Trailhead.

Finding the trailhead: From Chemult, drive west 12 miles on gravel Forest Road 9772, which is marked for Miller Lake. At the lake, continue to Digit Point Campground. Stay left and park in the picnic area north of the campground.

The hike: Follow the edge of the lake around Digit Point below the campground. An unmaintained trail takes you to the boat launch east of the campground. Find the marked trail, which is several dozen yards south of the boat ramp. Continue on the trail around the lake; this section isn't shown on the topographic map. At the east end of the lake, the trail follows the outlet stream east to the road. Turn left and walk the road about 50 yards, to the marked Maidu Lake Trail. Follow this trail around the north shore of the lake through ponderosa pine, Douglas-fir, and lodgepole pine forest. There are several small streams that enter the lake. At the west end of the lake, a sign marks the junction with the Miller Lake Trail. Turn left on this trail and continue about 0.7 mile to the picnic area and the trailhead.

Red Cone, Miller Lake.

General description:	A day hike or overnight backpack trip to the Cascade crest and the largest lake in the Mount Thielsen Wilderness.
Location:	About 12 miles west of Chemult.
Maps:	Miller Lake, Tolo Mountain, Burn Butte USGS; Rogue–Umpqua Divide, Boulder Creek, and Mount Thielsen wildernesses in Winema National Forest.
Difficulty:	Moderate.
Length:	5.4 miles round-trip.
Elevation:	5,630 to 6,200 feet.
Best season:	Summer and fall.
Permit:	Permit required for day and overnight hikes; self issue at trailhead.
For more information:	Chemult Ranger District, Winema National Forest.

See Map on Page 188

Key points:

0.0	Trailhead.
0.7	Turn left on the Maidu Lake Trail.
2.0	Cross the Pacific Crest National Scenic Trail.
2.7	Maidu Lake.

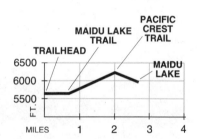

Duck at Maidu Lake.

Finding the trailhead: From Chemult, drive west 12 miles on gravel Forest Road 9772, which is marked for Miller Lake. At the lake, continue to Digit Point Campground. Stay left and park in the picnic area north of the campground.

The hike: From the left (west) end of the picnic area parking lot, follow the marked Miller Lake Trail along the lakeshore about 0.7 mile. Turn left (west) at the marked junction with the Maidu Lake Trail. The trail wanders through open lodgepole pine forest, then climbs a steep slope by traversing south at a very gentle grade. There are occasional views of Miller Lake to the east. Rounding a corner, the gradient becomes more gentle as the trail follows the upper valley toward the crest. Signs mark the junction with the Pacific Crest National Scenic Trail, which crosses at right angles. Continue straight ahead on the marked Maidu Lake Trail. The lake, a pleasant one and the largest in the Mount Thielsen Wilderness, is reached after about 0.6 mile.

75   TIPSOO PEAK

General description:	A day hike to a high summit overlooking the Mount Thielsen Wilderness.
Location:	About 84 miles east of Roseburg.
Maps:	Mount Thielsen USGS; Rogue–Umpqua Divide, Boulder Creek, and Mount Thielsen Wildernesses, Winema National Forest USDAFS.
Difficulty:	Moderate.
Length:	6.4 miles round trip.
Elevation:	6,520 to 8,034 feet.
Best season:	Summer and fall.
Permit:	Permit required for day and overnight hikes; self issue at trailhead.
For more information:	Diamond Lake Ranger District, Umpqua National Forest.

Key points:

0.0   Trailhead.
3.2   Tipsoo Peak.

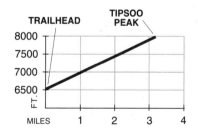

Finding the trailhead: From Roseburg drive about 79 miles east on Oregon Highway 138, then turn left on Forest Road 4733 (the Cinnamon Butte Road). This gravel road is also signed for Tipsoo Peak. After about 1.6

miles, the Cinnamon Butte Road goes left; continue straight until the road ends at the signed trailhead, 5.0 miles from the highway.

The hike: Although the trail climbs 1,500 feet, it does so at a very easy grade. It switchbacks through an open mountain hemlock forest, which becomes more open as you ascend. Several short switchbacks lead to a long traverse to the southeast, then more short switchbacks as the trail starts to pass through open parks and alpine meadows. A few western white pine and whitebark pine appear, but the forest is still predominantly mountain hemlock. As you near the summit, the trees become shorter and then stunted, a sure sign that timberline is near. The trail passes through a small saddle, then turns right and climbs steeply for a dozen yards to reach the summit ridge. The actual high point is at the east end of the ridge, marked by a U.S. Coast and Geodetic Survey benchmark, a brass cap set in the rock. The Three Sisters can be seen to the north, as can Diamond Peak. To the northeast, Miller and Maidu lakes sparkle in the forest. Spirelike Mount Thielsen dominates the view to the south, separated from our vantage point by Howlock Mountain and appealing alpine meadows.

ADDITIONAL TRAILS

The Pacific Crest National Scenic Trail runs south from a trailhead at Windigo Pass on Forest Road 90 and enters the Mount Thielsen Wilderness near Tolo Mountain. It crosses to the west slopes south of Tipsoo Peak and

Alpine parks south of Tipsoo Peak.

TIPSOO PEAK

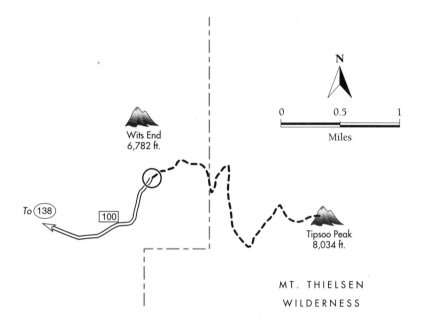

leaves the south end of the wilderness to enter Crater Lake National Park at the North Crater Trailhead on Oregon Highway 138.

Maidu Lake Trail continues past Maidu Lake down the North Umpqua River to the Kelsey Valley Trailhead on FR 958.

Mount Thielsen Trail starts from OR 138 and climbs to meet the Pacific Crest National Scenic Trail west of Mount Thielsen.

AFTERWORD

It doesn't take long for a hiker to begin to appreciate wild country. Although hiking in semi-urban settings can be pleasant, most natural settings are more enjoyable. The idea behind the wilderness conservation movement is to preserve the opportunity for primitive, non-motorized recreation and to protect wild plants and animals in their natural settings.

Aldo Leopold of the USDA Forest Service began to promote the idea of preserving wild country within the national forests in the 1920s. A few years later, the agency began designating formal wilderness and primitive areas. Roads and other permanent manmade structures were excluded from such areas, although trails and compatible activities were allowed, including hunting, fishing, grazing, and limited mining. Most of the lands within the national parks were also managed, though not formally designated, as wilderness. This protection was under the control of the land management agencies, which could rescind the wilderness designation at any time.

Congress decided to take the wilderness concept one step further when it passed the Wilderness Act in 1964, establishing the National Wilderness Preservation System. Most of the existing designated wilderness and primitive areas on the national forests were included in this new system. Since then, Congress has added many additional areas to our wilderness system, including lands managed by the National Park Service and the Bureau of Land Management, as well as the Forest Service.

While protecting roadless areas is vital, land managers are now looking at a larger picture—protection of entire, intact ecosystems. As we learn more about plant and animal habitats, we find that survival of individual species is linked to the health of other plants and animals as well as the overall quality of the air and water. Instead of protecting a few isolated wild areas and ignoring the consequences of unrestricted human activities on the rest of the land, we have to consider entire watersheds and forests and how proposed activities will affect them.

APPENDIX A: RESOURCES

CONSERVATION AND HIKING ORGANIZATIONS

Association of Forest Service
Employees for Environmental Ethics
P.O. Box 11615
Eugene, OR 97440
(541) 484-2692

Earth Island Institute
300 Broadway, Suite 28
San Francisco, CA 94133-3312
(415) 788-3666

National Audubon Society
700 Broadway
New York, NY 10003-9562
(212) 979-3000

National Wildlife Federation
8925 Leesburg Pike
Vienna, VA 22184
(800) 588-1650

Northwest Ecosystem Alliance
P.O. Box 2813
Bellingham, WA 98227
(360) 671-9950

Oregon League of
Conservation Voters
520 SW 6th Ave., Suite 701
Portland, OR 98204
(503) 224-4011

Oregon Natural
Resources Council
5825 North Greeley
Portland, OR 97217-4145
(503) 283-6343

Sierra Club
85 Second St., Second Floor
San Francisco, CA 94105-3441
(415) 977-5500

The Nature Conservancy
1815 North Lynn Street
Arlington, VA 22209
(703) 841-5300

Wilderness Society
900 Seventeenth St. NW
Washington, D.C. 20006
(202) 833-2300

CONSERVATION PUBLICATIONS

High Country News
P.O. Box 1090
Paonia, CO 81428
(970)-527-4898

PUBLIC AGENCIES

U.S. Geological Survey
Map Distribution Branch
Box 25286
Denver Federal Center
Denver, CO 80225

Deschutes National Forest
Supervisor's Office
1645 Highway 20 East
Bend, OR 97701
(541) 388-2715

Bend–Fort Rock
Ranger District
1230 NE 3rd., Suite A-262
Bend, OR 97701
(541) 388-5664

Crescent Ranger District
P.O. Box 208
Crescent, OR 97733
(541) 433-2234

Sisters Ranger District
P.O. Box 249
Sisters, OR 97759
(541) 549-5071

Newberry Crater National
Volcanic Monument
1230 NE 3rd., Suite A-262
 Bend, OR 97701
(541) 388-5664

Mount Hood National Forest
Supervisor's Office
16400 Champion Way
Sandy, OR 97055
(503) 668-1771

Estacada–Clackamas
Ranger District
595 NW Industrial Way
Estacada, OR 97023
(503) 630-6861

Umpqua National Forest
Supervisor's Office
P.O. Box 1008
2900 NW Stewart Parkway
Roseburg, OR 97470
(541) 676-6601

Diamond Lake Ranger District
2020 Toketee Ranger Station Rd.
Idleyld Park, OR 97447
(541) 498-2531

Willamette National Forest
Supervisor's Office
211 East 7th Ave.
Eugene, OR 97440,
(541) 465-6521

Blue River Ranger District
(off State Highway 126)
Blue River, OR 97413
(541) 822-3317

Detroit Ranger District
State Highway 22
Detroit, OR 97360
(mail address HC73
Box 321, Mill City, OR 97360)
(503) 854-3366

Lowell Ranger District
(off State Highway 58)
Lowell, OR 97452
(541) 937-2129

McKenzie Ranger District
State Highway 126
McKenzie Bridge
OR 97413
(541) 822-3381

Oakridge Ranger District
49098 Salmon Creek Rd.
Oakridge, OR 97463
(541) 782-2291

Rigdon Ranger District
49098 Salmon Creek Rd.
Oakridge, OR 97463
(541) 782-2283

Sweet Home Ranger District
3225 Highway 20
Sweet Home, OR 97386
(541) 367-5168

Winema National Forest
Supervisor's Office
2819 Dahlia Street
Klamath Falls, OR 97601
(541) 883-6714

Chemult Ranger District
P.O. Box 150
Chemult, OR 97731
(541) 365-7001

APPENDIX B: FURTHER READING

Aitkenhead, Donna Ikenberry. *Central Oregon Wilderness Areas*. Beaverton, Ore.: Touchstone Press, 1991.

Cissel, Diane, John Cissel, and Peter Eberhardt. *50 Old-Growth Day Hikes in the Willamette National Forest*. Eugene, Ore.: 1991.

Fletcher, Colin. *The Complete Walker III*. New York: Alfred A. Knopf, 1989.

Ashbaugh, James G., ed. *Pacific Northwest Geographical Perspectives*. Dubuque, Iowa: Kendal/Hunt Publishing Co., 1994.

Harris, Stephen L. *Fire Mountains of the West: The Cascade and Mono Lake Volcanoes*. Missoula, MT.: Mountain Press Publishing Company, 1988.

Hatton, Raymond R. *High Country of Central Oregon*. Portland, Ore.: Binford & Mort, 1980.

Ikenberry, Donna Lynn. *Hiking Oregon*. Helena, Mont.: Falcon Press, 1992.

Kricher, John C., and Gordon Morrison. *Ecology of Western Forests*. New York: Houghton Mifflin, 1993.

Perry, John, and Jane Perry. *Sierra Club Guide to the Natural Areas of Oregon and Washington*. San Fransico: Sierra Club Books, 1983.

Sullivan, William L. *100 Hikes in the Central Oregon Cascades*. Eugene, Ore.: Navillus Press, 1993.

Whitney, Stephen. *A Sierra Club Naturalist's Guide to the Pacific Northwest*. San Francisco: Sierra Club Books, 1989.

Wilkerson, James A. *Medicine for Mountaineering*. Seattle: The Mountaineers Press, Seattle, 1992.

Worth, Veryl M., and Harry S. Worth. *Early Days on the Upper Willamette*. Oakridge, Ore.: Fact Book Co., 1989.

APPENDIX C: HIKER'S CHECKLIST

This checklist may be useful for ensuring that nothing essential is forgotten. Of course, it contains far more items than are needed on any individual hiking trip.

ESSENTIALS

- [ ] water
- [ ] food
- [ ] rain/wind gear
- [ ] sunglasses
- [ ] sunscreen
- [ ] insect repellent
- [ ] knife
- [ ] lighter or other reliable fire starter
- [ ] map
- [ ] compass
- [ ] flashlight

FOOTWEAR

- [ ] boots
- [ ] extra socks
- [ ] boot wax
- [ ] camp shoes

SLEEPING

- [ ] tarp or tent with fly
- [ ] groundsheet
- [ ] sleeping pad
- [ ] sleeping bag

CLOTHING

- [ ] shirt
- [ ] pants
- [ ] extra underwear
- [ ] swimsuit
- [ ] walking shorts
- [ ] belt or suspenders
- [ ] jacket or parka
- [ ] gloves or mittens
- [ ] sun hat
- [ ] watch cap or balaclava
- [ ] sweater
- [ ] bandanna

COOKING

- [ ] stove
- [ ] fuel
- [ ] stove maintenance kit
- [ ] cooking pot(s)
- [ ] cup
- [ ] bowl or plate
- [ ] utensils
- [ ] pot scrubber
- [ ] plastic water bottles
- [ ] collapsible water containers

FOOD

- [ ] cereal
- [ ] bread
- [ ] crackers
- [ ] cheese
- [ ] margarine
- [ ] dry soup
- [ ] packaged dinners
- [ ] snacks
- [ ] hot chocolate
- [ ] tea
- [ ] powdered milk
- [ ] powdered drink mixes

MISCELLANEOUS

- [ ] fishing gear
- [ ] photographic gear
- [ ] candle lantern
- [ ] toilet paper
- [ ] trowel
- [ ] binoculars
- [ ] trash bags
- [ ] notebook and pencils
- [ ] field guides
- [ ] book or game
- [ ] dental and personal items
- [ ] towel
- [ ] water purification
      tablets or filter
- [ ] car key
- [ ] watch
- [ ] calendar

EMERGENCY/REPAIR

- [ ] first-aid kit
- [ ] snakebite kit
- [ ] nylon cord
- [ ] plastic bags
- [ ] wallet or ID card
- [ ] coins for phone calls
- [ ] space blanket
- [ ] emergency fishing gear
- [ ] signal mirror
- [ ] pack parts
- [ ] stove parts
- [ ] tent parts
- [ ] flashlight bulbs, batteries
- [ ] scissors
- [ ] safety pins

PACKING

- [ ] backpack
- [ ] day pack
- [ ] fanny pack

NAVIGATION

- [ ] maps
- [ ] compass
- [ ] GPS receiver

CAR

- [ ] extra water
- [ ] extra food
- [ ] extra clothes

ABOUT THE AUTHOR

Bruce Grubbs has been hiking, cross-country skiing, and climbing in the American West for more than thirty years. He has participated in several technical first ascents of summits in the Grand Canyon, as well as numerous long backpack trips. He has explored most of Arizona's wilderness areas, as well as many places that are not officially protected. Trips out of state to explore the West are an annual treat. Grubbs is the author of three other FalconGuides, *Hiking Northern Arizona, Hiking Nevada,* and *Hiking Arizona* (with Stewart Aitchison). He spent four summers on a fire lookout for the USDA Forest Service and seven more seasons fighting fires for the Forest Service and the Bureau of Land Management. For several years he was an active partner in a mountain shop selling outdoor gear.

At present, Grubbs is a charter pilot and a computer consultant, as well as an outdoor writer and photographer. He lives in Flagstaff, Arizona.